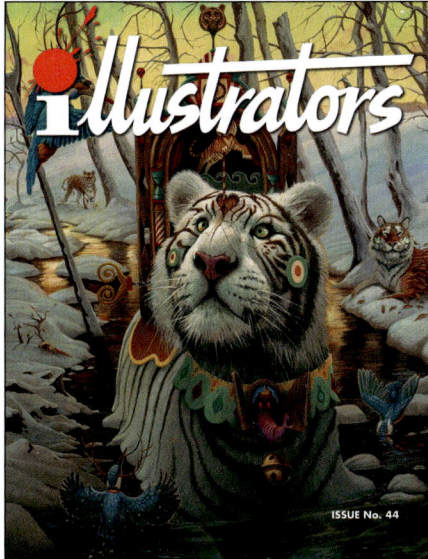

Front cover: Dulk
Back cover: William Hogarth

Illustrators
The Book Palace
Jubilee House
Bedwardine Road
Crystal Palace
London SE19 3AP

Email: IQ@bookpalace.com
Web: www.bookpalace.com
Tel: 020 8768 0022
(From overseas +44 20 8768 0022)

Publisher: Geoff West
gw@bookpalace.com
Editor, Writer & Designer: Diego Cordoba
Consultant Editors: Peter Richardson, Richard Sheaf
Website: Paul Tanner
Subscriptions & Distribution: Dylan Doodleman
Advertising: ads@bookpalace.com

illustrators ISBN 978-1-913548-54-4
ISSN 2052-6520
Issue 44 Spring 2024
Copyright © 2024 by The Book Palace Ltd.

Produced with Affinity Creative Software

illustrators is published quarterly.
Back issues from £25 plus postage
4 issue subscriptions (with 4 free digital issues)
UK £80 POST FREE
EU/USA/CAN £98 POST FREE
ROW £110 POST FREE

Trade Orders: IQ@bookpalace.com

Printed in England by Gomer Press

ISSUE No. 44

CONTENTS

EDITORIAL

WHAT'S THE DIFFERENCE BETWEEN ART AND ILLUSTRATION? The first is done to evoke an emotion, the second is commissioned to promote a product, concept or theme. However, aren't both done by artists? After all weren't Michelangelo, Leonardo and Raphael simply illustrators working for the Catholic church? We start off with an artist, Antonio Segura (who signs his work as Dulk), who began literally in the streets, as an urban artist creating murals, but whose paintings and murals remain personal and immediately identifiable.

Next we go back three centuries into the world of William Hogarth, a British painter, portraitist and engraver who found success with his personal moral images depicting the fortunes and failures within 18th century English society. He found inspiration amongst the streets of London and its population. He made prints of his paintings himself, pretty much as Gustave Doré did (*see **illustrators** No. 17*), which were more popular than his original paintings (again, as with Doré).

Coming back to present-day England, we find the truly original and psychedelic artwork of Murugiah (by way of Sri Lanka). Working mostly in the digital domain, his very personal work has graced the covers and interiors of magazines, been presented as posters but is also displayed on window panes, murals and canvas.

We then go down the rabbit hole and explore the world of AI. Will this really replace human illustrators? Read all about it and find out.

On a different topic we meet and check the dark and phantasmagorical artwork of Yin Xin He, a young Vietnamese artist living in Germany.

Finally in our Gallery section we present some samples from the last Tarzan story Russ Manning did for the European market. His four European Tarzan books are long due for a reprint in English.

Enjoy! **DC**

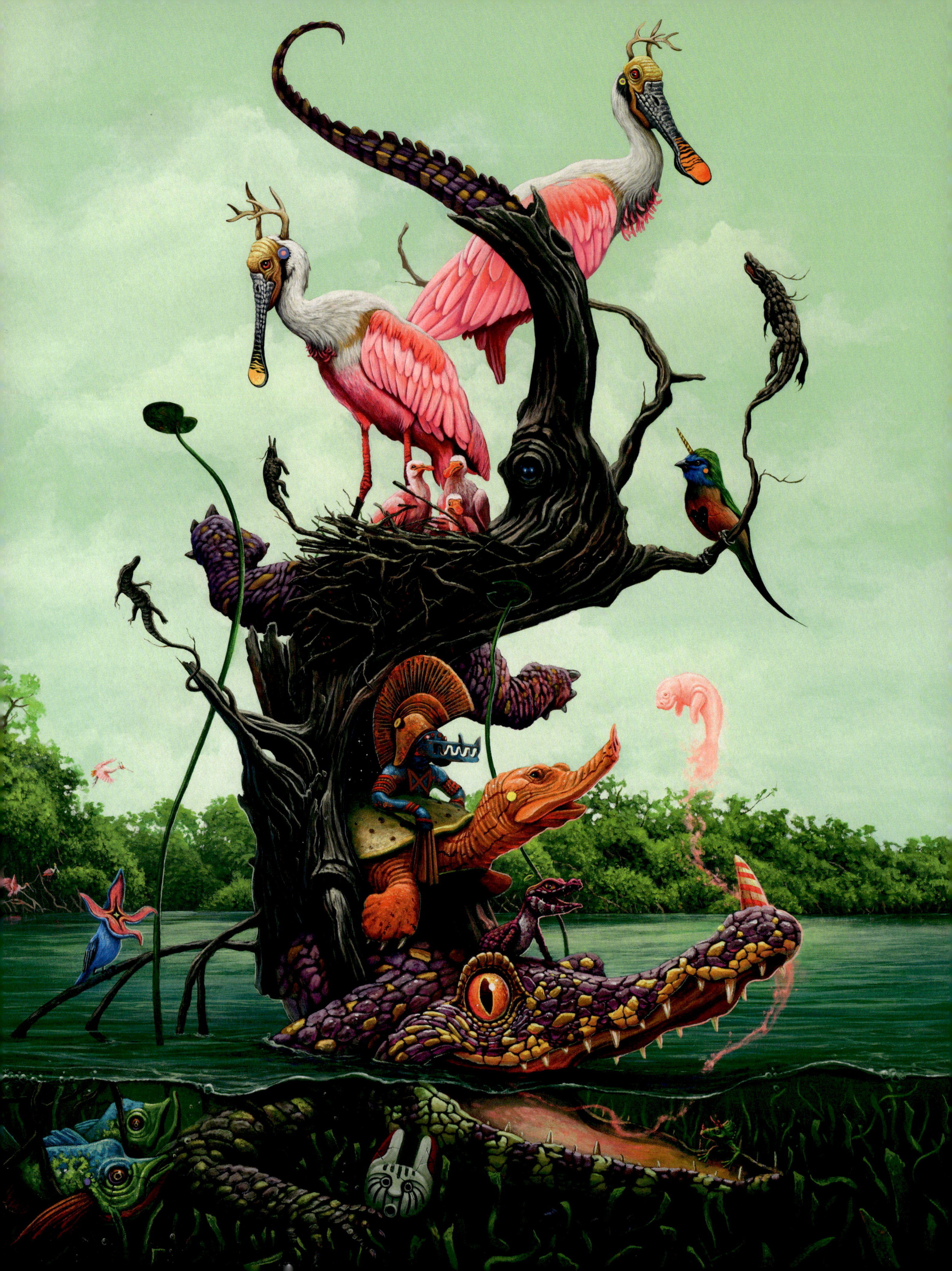

Dulk: from street art to art galleries

An artist of multiple talents, Dulk began creating graffiti in the streets and now his paintings are exhibited in museums and art galleries and his murals are all over the world. Diego Cordoba sat down with him recently to discuss his work.

FACING PAGE: *Everglades*, acrylics on canvas, 2023.
BELOW: *Archipelago*, acrylics on canvas, 2021.

For the Spanish pop surrealist artist known as Dulk—his work covering everything from urban art and murals, to paintings and sculptures—the boundaries between art and illustration are closely intertwined. "I simply illustrate what I like," he says. He doesn't necessarily work for a specific client instead he creates a series of paintings with a strong ecological conviction, defending the ecosystems that affect its most vulnerable species. All this is represented in an almost surrealistic way, yet not devoid of a certain degree of humour. "I try

BELOW: *Denali*, acrylics on canvas, 2023. Danali, also known as Mount McKinley, is the highest mountain peak in North America. This painting also forms part with 'Kenai Fjords' and 'Glacier Bay', related to the project on the region of Alaska, its animals and fauna. Parts of the Native American culture is also present here.

to caricature the animals in the event I'm showing," he explains. His paintings, whether ironic or critical, also show a *savoir-faire* and intrinsic knowledge of the animals he depicts. We can see that a lot of research has gone into painting the animals and the environment they live in. The fact that he creates them on walls all over the world (and on canvas and sculptures, too), makes both the images and its creator immediately recognisable, and

form an integral part of his unique and vivid imagination.

Born in Valencia, Spain, in 1983, Antonio Segura Donat, as a child, was witness to the aviary his father managed. The many birds there inspired his artistic talents as he sketched them in notebooks and drew them on paper. The animal encyclopaedias at home had him searching for all sort of animals which also fired up his imagination. Although he had the talent to follow an artistic career, he knew it was a difficult path to pursue, especially if you wanted to earn a living with it, so he first chose a career in economics. At the same time, due to his artistic talents, a friend persuaded him to tackle the walls of certain premises they frequented as many other street artists did. His friend suggested he use the name of 'Dulk' (pronounced 'doolk') as his signature. The name stuck, and shortly after his name and images were on walls. Starting to get a certain amount of recognition in the urban art world, Segura abandoned his studies in economics after a year-and-a-half, and instead switched to learn illustration and then study graphic design at the University of Valencia.

After a stint spent doing graffiti on walls and illustrations for many magazines (and even working in animated films designing characters), he decided to create his own art. At his first solo show in Italy he experimented with his animal paintings, and after the success of this show, decided to concentrate on that aspect of his artwork.

Today he is an all-purpose artist, dividing his time between creating murals, paintings and sculptures. His main focus being his animals in peril set in a very colourful biological environment. It is indeed the fabulous colours that first attracts the viewer's attention, and then the animals he depicts so life-like, mostly in incongruous situations. We may find a rhinoceros with a glass horn, a toucan with a transparent beak, a hippopotamus as a rocky shelter or a sea-horses merry-go-round, among the many other circumstances his animals live on canvasses or walls. His naturalistic worlds are depicted through a phantasmagorical eye yet within a tragic-comic landscape full of detail (bringing to mind the work of Hieronymus Bosch—if he painted animals only), inviting the viewer to dive into that colourful, surrealistic world.

I met Dulk last year, a couple of days before he went to South Africa on a mural commission. The following is the conversation we had about his work.

IQ: Let's start from the beginning. Do you remember when you first started drawing?
Dulk: I don't remember the exact date, but I know I was very young, just a child…
IQ: Well, all children like drawing, but what was it that inspired you to draw? Was it something in particular?
Dulk: Well, no, not really. There wasn't anything particular. I remember I liked drawing animals. My father had many birds, he ran an aviary, and I was drawing them as a child. We also had many books about animals, with pictures inside that I would copy, either by drawing over them or simply using them as reference. I can't really say why I began drawing. I just know I liked it…

ABOVE: *Yellowstone*, acrylics on canvas, 2023. Although better known as a National Park with its unique hydrothermal and geological features, it was also the land where the buffalo roamed free, and now are just a puff of smoke.

FACING PAGE: *Sequoia*, acrylics on canvas, 2023. Even though Dulk shows animals close to or already extinct—to draw the viewer's attention, he also lets his imagination run free.

IQ: Did you ever think you wanted to be an artist later on in life?

Dulk: Well, I remember the images from the books I was telling you about. The illustrations inside were done by different artists, and I always thought I'd love doing something like that: illustrate books about animals. It was the first time I thought, "I'd love to do something like that," and I was only a child at the time. I don't remember how old I was.

IQ: Where the books mainly about birds?

Dulk: All sort of animals, but done in a more scientific way. More realistically.

IQ: After finishing school, did you study art?

Dulk: Well, after finishing school I went to study economics. I remained there for about a year and a half, and afterwards I found out it wasn't for me. I mean, I loved art, but at the same time I knew it would be very hard to make a living from that, so I decided not to study art… before the year and half I was telling you about. After that I started studying illustration. I was around 19 years old at the time and it was the period when I had also begun doing graffiti in the streets. I started to appreciate art more, and also took it more seriously. So all this came around at the same time—when I began to study illustration and getting to know other people who also liked drawing, because as I child I didn't know anyone who liked drawing as much as I did. This opened the doors into the art world; getting to know other like-minded people with the same interests as I had.

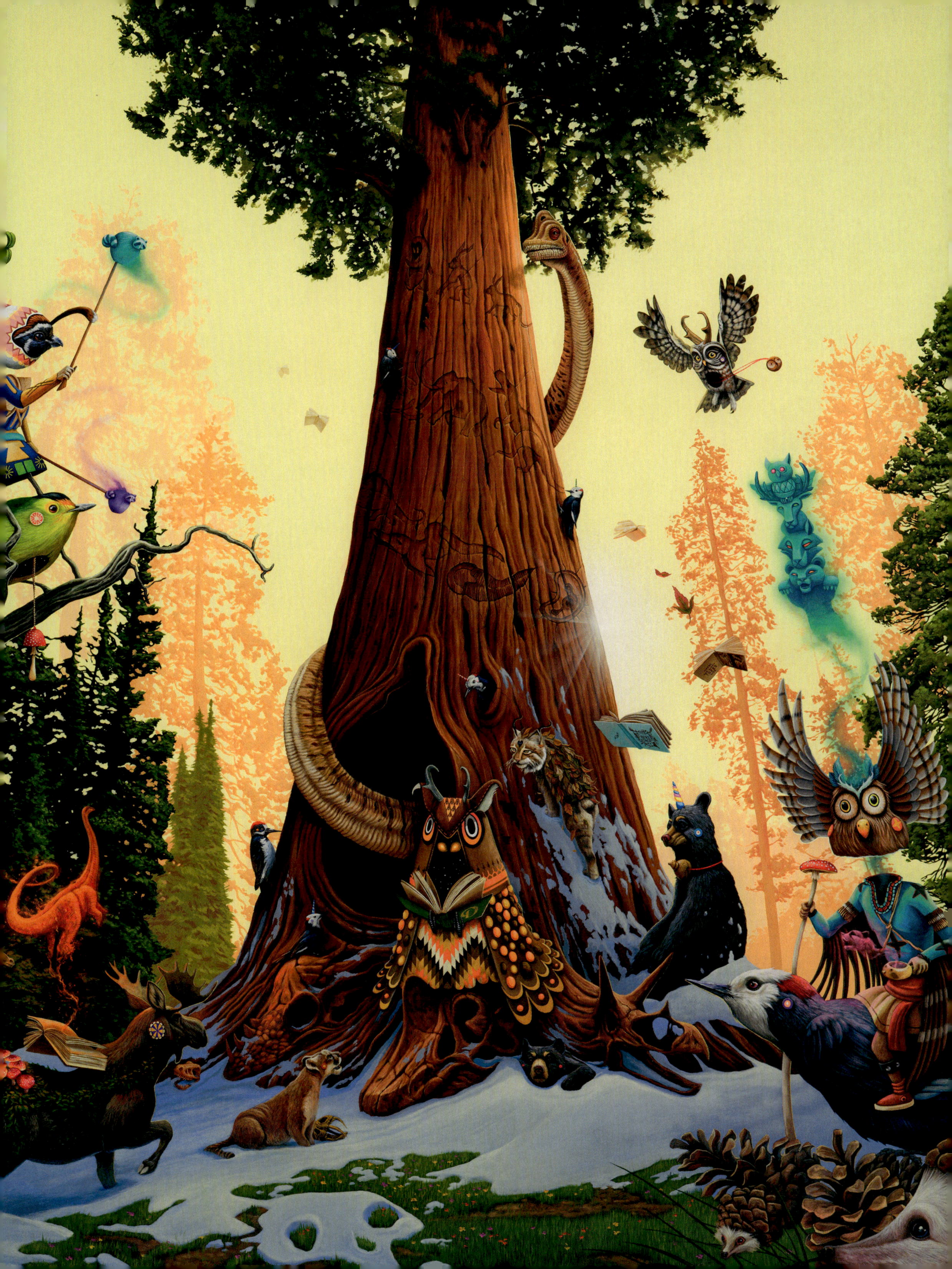

IQ: What were the first works you did in the art field? Did you start out working for free?

Dulk: While I was studying, I had already began to paint on the walls of some premises, the fronts of buildings or on the blinds of windows. In illustration, I did much work for free, in magazines. My first remunerated work… uhh, I don't remember when it began. I did a lot of work for free.

IQ: So right now you live from the paintings you sell through art galleries and the murals you do?

Dulk: Right now, yes. But before I started doing my paintings, I lived from advertising illustrations. I also designed characters for an animation studio. I worked on some movies, on the screenplays and, uh, well, a little of everything. For some publishers as well… but at the same time, I also worked on what I liked, which was more personal and focused on the animals, nature and the environment. For every commercial work I did, I also worked in parallel on what I liked.

When I got the chance to do a solo show in Europe, all the paintings got sold. The same happened with another solo show I did in America. Since then I've been focusing more on art than illustration. And now I live from my art: paintings, murals and sculptures. Some graphic work as well…

IQ: I was wondering if you have also painted human figures, because in all your work we only see animals.

Dulk: Yes, I have, but much less than animals. When it was commercial work, I adapted to what I was asked for. But now I have developed my own style and concentrate on what I like, so if I get a commission it's usually around what I do.

Continued on page 14

FACING PAGE: *Mediterrània*, acrylics on canvas, 2023. Closer to his home, Dulk brings us a view on animals living in the Mediterranean. "I try to caricature the animals to give them more personality."

ABOVE: *Kenai Fjords*, acrylics on canvas, 2023. We find this region with outflowing glaciers and coastal fjords and islands in Alaska. Again, Native American symbolism is also present.

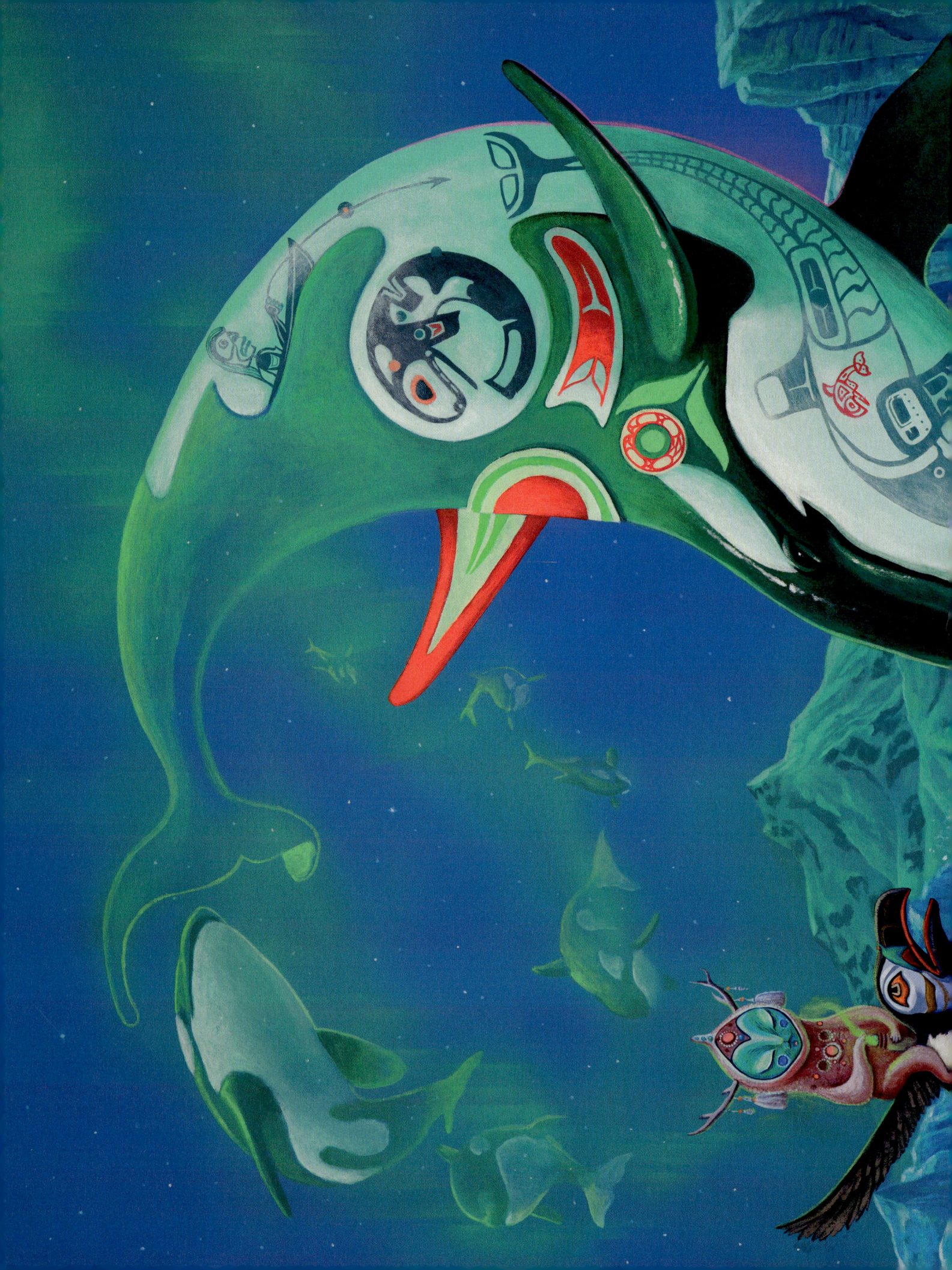

PREVIOUS PAGES LEFT: *Smoky Mountains*, acrylics on canvas, 2023.

PREVIOUS PAGE RIGHT: *Biscayne*, acrylics on canvas, 2023.

ABOVE: *Glacier Bay*, acrylics on canvas, 2023.

FOLLOWING PAGES: *Who Is the Next?*, acrylics on wood panel, 2022. Large size painting at the Promenade Saint-Catherine in Bordeaux, France, to celebrate the opening of 'Stories and One Root OneArtists' exhibition. "Orang-utan (man of the forest) is one of the most endangered animals worldwide and I wanted to show him in the next step of a books tower formed by already extinct animals from Indonesia surrounded by some of the most iconic birds of their habitat."

Continued from page 9

IQ: Getting back to what you mentioned earlier, the movies you worked on were in the animation field?

Dulk: Yes. I worked on the screenplays, creating the characters, objects and so on.

IQ: Did any of them get made?

Dulk: One did, the other was in stop-motion and is still in the production process. It's a very slow process working in stop-motion. They have spent like five, six years working on that movie.

IQ: How did you get invited to your solo shows in art galleries? Had you already worked on something prior to it, and done your animal paintings?

Dulk: My first solo show was in Rome. Earlier on my paintings were more caricatural with the representation of the animals. They were done in a more graphic, caricature-like style. Flatter, uh… It was an experiment at the time, as I didn't quite know what I wanted to do with my animals. But this gave me a chance to be more focused on what I wanted to do personally. So I was finding my way into what I do now.

IQ: Your choice of images also brings forth a message. The way you show your animals, like bears with the snow melting over or around them… but at the same time, we see the vestiges of human kind in their environments,

sometimes with sections of a building forming part of the animal's body. In other words, your paintings come with some sort of message.

Dulk: Well, yes, but I try not to make it too obvious. It's for the viewer to create his own story on the image he views. The colours and the environment also captivates the viewer. It's sort of like looking through a window into reality and imagination at the same time. In the end the message corresponds to reality: the destruction of the ecosystem and the species' extinction. I try to find a metaphor to what happens to each species I show, to make them visually attractive and powerful all at once.

IQ: The message you convey, for example, on a rhinoceros with a glass horn, as if to indicate how humans hunt them only for their horns—

Dulk: How fragile they are and yet powerful at the same time. How close they are to extinction. For every animal I depict, I try to fusion them with nature, to give them that

FACING PAGE: *Green Dream*, mural (in Belgium), 2023. "This is a mural in the heart of the city of Brussels, in a new green area over the Mairesse Garden in Saint-Gilles. The idea behind all of this is bringing green where you've never seen it before."

BELOW: Dulk at work on the 'Green Dream' mural.

THESE PAGES: *Roots*, mural in Miami (Florida), 2023. "This mural is inspired by the Everglades, a natural region of tropical wetlands in the southern portion of Florida. I'd been to their National Park several times, photographing their incredible wildlife. When I was invited to paint this mural in this iconic place, I didn't hesitate to create an image based on my original pictures of the region."

sensation that they are ephemeral and vigorous as well.

IQ: *Do you do a lot of research on your animals, with photography and visiting the places where they live?*

Dulk: Yes. Well, I try as much as possible to travel, but haven't been able to go everywhere. I'm still young…

IQ: *Nowadays with the internet you can see pictures of animals from all over the world and in their natural habitat.*

Dulk: Totally! But it's also true that when you see them in person in their natural habitat, the sensation is very powerful. When you experience seeing the animals in the

Continued on page 24

The 2021 Fallas: A year and a half of work gone up in smoke in 10 minutes!

The Fallas is a traditional celebration held annually in Valencia (Spain) in commemoration of Saint Joseph, the patron saint of carpenters. The five main days are celebrated between March 15th to 19th every year, while the Mascleta, a pyrotechnic spectacle, takes place every day from March 1st to 19th. The fireworks are celebrated all around the city, with the biggest event held in the main square of the city. Fireworks are put inside large-sized *ninots* ('dolls' or 'puppets' in Valencian), sort of papier-mâché figures that represent important personalities or fantastical ones. For the biggest of these sculpted figures the city usually asks a local artist to build it, and for 2021 they asked Dulk (although due to the pandemic, the Fallas actually took place a year later). He based his concept on his painting 'Protect What You Love' (below), representing in its foreground a polar bear that is melting, along with various other species of animals.

Dulk prepared a 23-metres high sculpture that took him and his team over a year to accomplish. The interior structure was made of wood and cardboard, and the exterior was covered in polythene and papier-mâché, and later painted over. The inside was filled with fireworks and on the last day of the celebration, it was set on fire. The whole structure burned down in less than 10 minutes!

"It was spectacular," Dulk said, as he saw his year and a half labour on the largest sculpture he ever built go up in flames.

RIGHT: *Protect What You Love*, acrylics on canvas, 2021. For the *falla* he was going to build, Dulk came up with this idea, showing a polar bear melting and carrying on his shoulders various animals he had represented in his previous paintings. The message the painting (and later sculpture) addressed was the urgency to protect endangered species, some of which are either extinct or near extinction.

FACING PAGE: Graphite sketch showing the back of the image on the painting, where we see part of the interior structure of what will become the sculpture. The sheer weight of building such a gigantic sculpture, meant that a wooden frame had to hold it in place. The whole project, from initial idea to final work, took about a year and half to accomplish. To mount the structure in the main square of the city, it took a team of nearly 20 men three weeks to put in place!

FACING PAGE: We see the various stages of building the sculpture, which was done by sections which later had to be transported and mounted in the main square of the city of Valencia. The whole structure was supported by a wooden frame (top right), and later melded over with polythene and papier-mâché. On the image at the bottom we see the gigantic sculpture in the middle of the town square. It was 23-metres high, making it the largest sculpture Dulk has ever created!

THIS PAGE: To celebrate the *falla*, the sculpture Dulk prepared was filled with fireworks which were fired on the last day of the celebration and then set on fire. It burned to the ground in less than 10 minutes among flames and fireworks shooting out from within its frame! All this was done, obviously, under the close scrutiny from the local fire department service.

Photos: Carlos Segura and Jesús Amable Gil

Continued from page 19

open and in their own environment, you try to get that same sensation on the work you are doing with every detail you add. You're living that sensation once again as you work on the painting. Even if people don't know it, I do. I like when people notice that what I'm depicting actually exists. This led to collaborations with associations connected in helping the environment. If our work can help, maybe not to end the problem, but to find a way to lessen the problem, it's always gratifying. We have worked that way with some foundations, and we will try to participate as best we can with any possible help.

IQ: Even if your paintings may seem surrealistic, your animals are painted very realistically. We can see you have either observed them closely or studied them carefully.

Dulk: Yes, but even so I try to caricature them as well, to give them more personality. I also like to diversify and use many different species. That's the part I enjoy the most, working on different species individually, trying to capture their essence as close as possible, and at the same time create a different story for each of them.

IQ: Let's talk about the technical stuff now. You work mainly in acrylics.

Dulk: Yes, and on canvas.

IQ: And what about your murals—what do you use?

Dulk: The same, synthetic colours. Acrylics also, but for facades.

IQ: How do the murals happen? Do they contact you?

Paintings from the Legacy Solo Show in Los Angeles (California):

BELOW LEFT: *Summit,* acrylics on canvas, 2018.

BELOW RIGHT: *Ageless,* acrylics on wood panel, 2018.

FACING PAGE: Carousel, acrylics on canvas, 2018.

Dulk: Yes. Usually for festivals, sometimes associations, or city councils. There are many organisations who ask to have murals created in their cities. It's something that has become very popular. I began doing graffiti as a child, but then it got more serious. At first these were done in groups, but the first big mural I did solo was in Copenhagen (Denmark), about ten years or so ago. Since then I have been doing murals all over the world. It's something very nice because it permits me to travel and meet new people. It's also very satisfactory, because it's an art for the people in each place, and anyone can see it. It's interesting to receive some feedback. It's something I appreciate very much. I do the murals in parallel to my work at the studio…

IQ: And something for everyone in the world to appreciate.

Dulk: Yes, it's for everyone.

IQ: For those murals do you have an assistant or something, because it's a lot of work for one person only (laughs).

Dulk: Yes (*smiles*). Here in the studio we are five, and for the murals I usually have a second person who helps me.

IQ: Tell me how do you work on the murals? Do you see the place first and then come up with an idea? Take us through the whole process of creating a mural.

Dulk: First of all is the place where they want the mural and then seeing the wall where they want it on. Then the mural must have a relation with the place I'm going to

work in. And obviously, it centres around with what I do with the fauna but in relation to the place.

For example, this Friday I'm leaving for South Africa to do a mural for a foundation that protects the animals over there. I'm telling you this because it's recent. I have been investigating about the place I'm going to. It happens to be one of the three places in the world where you can find the white shark. Some years ago they found out that the killer whales have been finishing with them. The orcas attack the sharks only to eat their livers and leave their corpses to rot. Each time they are killing more and more sharks, and they are finishing with them. The white sharks are a very typical species of the region, so the mural will be around that. I read about it in the *National Geographic* and thought it was a very powerful situation, and a source for an image. As to the process, you do the drawing on the wall and then fill it in with colour.

THESE PAGES: *Natural Challenge*, mural done last year in Cape Town, South Africa, for SeaWalls, a foundation preserving endangered species. Dulk in company of Maria Ivanco who assisted him with the mural. "South Africa is one of the most famous places to find great white sharks. I love those ocean predators, but I had never painted them on a mural before. Then I started to investigate about the white shark situation in Cape Town, and discovered that two orcas, Port and Starboard, had been killing sharks in the area and eating their livers and leaving their bodies behind. In the mural I wanted to capture the essence of this battle between two ocean giants, a confrontation resembling Godzilla agaist King Kong. But beyond that, it also highlighted the crisis that affects other local species, such as the penguins. White sharks' primary source in their food chain are the sea lions, who in turn eat penguins. However, with the number of white sharks decreasing, the sea lions are increasing and this is breaking the ecosystem and creating a new threat to the African penguins, who have now become an endangered species."

IQ: Do you sketch something on the wall with graphite or what?

Dulk: No, no—

IQ: Because I was thinking that the simplest way would be to take a picture of the wall and then in Photoshop sketch an image over the photo, to give you an idea of what you will do.

Dulk: Yes, more or less. I begin by doing a collage with pictures of the different animals I want to use, and from that I do a tight pencil sketch of the image as a whole. From there I scan the image into Photoshop and superimpose it over a picture of the wall. I also add digitally some of the colours to get an idea of what I need, and from there on you order the colours and do the work on the wall.

IQ: Now here's something that I don't know if you are aware of or not, but after you've done your mural there will always be some smart aleck who will either scribble his name or doodle something over your work. Is this something you think adds to the work or, on the contrary, spoils it.

Dulk: Completely spoils it! But it's something you can't do anything about. If you think too much about it, you'd never do a mural. So you finish your work and leave, and not think about it. But there are many other things that can happen: the wall may fall, humidity may wreck it… I've had them all. In the end, it's an ephemeral art. It won't last forever, alas. But the moment you do it, it's very powerful, you know. Just do it and… nothing more. Everything eventually comes to an end.

IQ: You have also work in sculpture…

Dulk: Yes, I do the designs, in graphite or digitally, and there's a team that builds them in 3D, and I supervise it. Doing them here would be impossible with all the other work I do.

Photos: Yoshi Travel Films

IQ: You also built a giant sculpture in Spain that was later burnt.

Dulk: Yes, it was for the Fallas of Valencia, where I come from. Every year the city celebrates the coming of Spring as a festival called 'falla' (*pronounced 'fah-yah'*). Anciently, to celebrate Spring, the inhabitants would burn all the belongings they didn't need anymore. Nowadays, what they do are giant papier-mâché sculptures and spread them all over the city, and later they burn them. In the centre of the city there is a main one for which they hire a different artist every year. In 2020 they chose me to build the principal sculpture. It was 23 metres (75 feet) high and it took about a year and half to build. The structure was held together with wood and cardboard, and was later covered in polythene and *papier-mâché*. The main figure was of a polar bear with the snow melting around him, serving as a metaphor to the climate changes and global warming, and since it was burnt later on, it served perfectly to the message I wanted to convey. As I said, it took a year and a half to build and it was consumed by fire in less than 10 minutes. But it was spectacular!

IQ: There's something I haven't asked you yet, and we can end our conversation here, and that's about the artists that have inspired you or that you admire.

Dulk: I love El Bosco (*Spanish name given to Hieronymus Bosch*), Brueghel and the flemish artists. Of the surrealists I love Dalí and Magritte… and many others. But these were my main influences. 🔴

● *You can visit Dulk's webpage:* **Dulk.es** *He is also present on Facebook and Instagram. A book collecting some of his recent work came out in 2022 and can be ordered directly from his website.*

ABOVE: Dulk at work on *Natural Challenge* mural in Cape Town, South Africa, November 2023.

OUT NOW !

Author and Editor: Peter Richardson

Contents: The ultimate guide to the US artists who made Warren's monster mags the best in the business. With the aid of friends, family, fans, historians and the artists themselves, we have assembled the compelling stories of the talented team who worked throughout the golden years of Warren Publishing. With an introduction by legendary film director Guillermo Del Toro, we guarantee this is a book no true monster fan will want to be without. Limited to 1500 copies worldwide and 120 slipcased sets containing the full set of 3 Book Palace Warren hardcovers (The Spanish Artists, The History and The US Artists) only available direct from the publisher and including a signed Vampirella print by Joe Jusko, the US's premier Vampirella artist. We advise reserving your copy early.

Publisher: Book Palace Books

Number of pages: 400

Format: Hardcover; Full colour illustrations

Size: 9" x 11" (216mm x 280mm)

ISBN: 978-1-913548-50-6

The LINE of BEAUTY
W. H. 1745

William Hogarth

The artist-engraver whose satirical eye exposed all the ups and downs of British social mores during the 18th century. His series of tableaus sequentially telling the stories of individual citizens trying to make it into the upper echelons of society proved incredibly popular when sold as prints.

MANY ART CRITICS TRY TO DIFFERENTIATE ILLUSTRATION FROM FINE ART. One is done for commercial reasons on behalf of a client, the other is a personal inner expression of the artist's imagination. However, artistically speaking, what's the difference? As Mort Kunstler (*see* **illustrators** *issues 17 and 30 respectively*) once said, "There's no difference

FACING PAGE: *The Painter and his Pug*, oil on canvas, 1745. A self-portrait with his pug, Trump. Although it seems Hogarth is posing with his pug, in reality the dog is sitting in front of a portrait of the artist. The books below the portrait are by Shakespeare, John Milton and Jonathan Swift, three of Hogarth's favourite writers.

BELOW: *A Harlot's Progress, Plate I*, etching and engraving, 1732. Part of a series of prints telling the story of the fall and destruction of a young and innocent country girl coming to the city to earn a living and ending in prostitution. These prints of the original paintings turned Hogarth into a huge success among the population avid for scabrous stories.

in the art world between illustrators and painters. Painters such as Leonardo or Michelangelo both worked under commission for the clergy and were paid to create religious paintings. Which isn't different from what illustrators do for magazines, where they are commissioned by editors to create paintings for their publications." Kunstler, a prolific illustrator from the men's adventure magazines in the 1950s, has since become one of the most important American historical painters, with his work shown in art galleries and museums.

An artist who best epitomises the link between illustration and painting was the 18th century engraver, painter, raconteur extraordinaire, William Hogarth, who through a series of tableaus would tell the story of an English rake—a fashionable, no-good upper middle-class young man who squanders away what little inheritance he possesses on gambling, drinking and women of ill-repute— or of some poor country girl trying to make a living in the big city resorting to prostitution. Never has an artist taken such a pitiless (yet darkly humorous) view into the mores of British society. Violence, poverty, prostitution, drunkenness and the pursuit of luxury were among the themes this printmaker born and raised in London, chose to share with his public, becoming one of the foremost social and political satirists of his time.

Best remembered for his 'modern moral subjects', a series of pictures telling the story of a person and his or her life within London society, William Hogarth was born to a poor middle-class family in 1697. As a youngster his interest laid more in the street life and local fairs in and around London—where he sketched and mimicked the characters he saw—than in his schooling. At the age of 15 he took an apprenticeship as a silversmith, learning the craft of plate engraving, although he relied mostly on his unorthodox methods, as he had a propensity to doing the exact opposite of what he was told. When his father, a minor classics scholar and schoolmaster, died prematurely in 1718, young William had to take care of his family.

FACING PAGE: *A Harlot's Progress, Plate IV*, etching and engraving, 1732. The original paintings of this series were unfortunately destroyed in a fire in 1795. Luckily Hogarth had turned them into prints as well. The reason why Hogarth's engravings look so great, is because he did them himself. In this particular print we see our story's main character, M. (Moll or Mary?) Hackabout, who has been imprisoned in Bridewell Prison for soliciting, beating on some hemp with a mallet. In this brutal 'house of correction', among the many disreputable characters, we see the woman behind Moll stealing an item from her dress while mocking her fashionable condition, a prison guard holding a stick to beat his prisoners, and at the far right a woman killing lice on her knee.

At the age of 23 he started his own shop, mainly engraving coats of arms, shop bills, and designing plates for books. He also attended private drawing classes on St. Martin's Lane, where along with the other students, he sketched from casts and live models. Nonetheless, he found the lessons distasteful, considering all the students were doing was merely 'copying'. He believed the best way to learn how to draw was to experience it from real life, and go out onto the streets and sketch what he saw.

Hogarth was more of a realist than a fantasist, and he would spend hours observing what was around him (in the streets of London), committing all he saw to his mind, creating what he had seen from memory once he got back at home. Although he was earning a living with his shop, he wasn't satisfied with his work. Admiring the work of Sir James Thornhill, a painter of historical subjects who worked in the Italian Baroque style—and held the post of serjeant painter to the king (and had been the first British painter to ever be knighted)—Hogarth decided to take lessons from him. Thornhill had recently opened a sketching school at his own home. Although Hogarth adhered to Thornhill's way of thinking on the vitality of native art and the social respectability of the artist, in the first major work he presented ('Masquerades and Operas', published in 1724 independently of the booksellers) he attacked the contemporary way of thinking, something that put him at odds with the 'experts'. Hogarth was already showing signs of being completely independent from other artists or what the experts considered was the right way to paint. He was a deft oil painter, even though he was almost self-taught, eschewing current trends in painting, although he was inspired by the French Rococo style during his early painting stages.

Adamant about what he sketched or painted, in 1728 Hogarth brought a lawsuit against Joshua Morris, a tapestry weaver who had rejected a painting he had ordered from him on the grounds that it wasn't finished when Hogarth delivered it. Seeking public

FACING PAGE: *Strolling Actress Dressing in a Barn*, etching and engraving, second state of four, 1738. In 1737, 'The Act against Strolling Players' made it illegal for plays to be performed outside London and Westminster without a licence. The troupe we see in this image is giving its last performance before the Act takes place. Although the play appears to rely on classic theatrical tropes with goddesses, sirens, cherubs and demons, all the actors seem rather bawdy (the woman in the centre is already half-naked), drinking beer or mead and jesting.

ABOVE: *The Enraged Musician*, etching and engraving, 1741. An effete violinist, probably a court musician, is enraged by the street noise from the London underclass. It was Hogarth's attention to detail that made his prints extremely popular. This image in particular, has inspired many other artists covering the same subject.

FACING PAGE: *Beer Street*, etching and engraving, 1751. First of two prints concerning the high consumption of gin among working classes in the 18th century. The two plates ('Gin Lane' on the following page) were were a response to the government's attempts, via the Gin Act of 1751, to control the sale of alcohol. As shown in this image, beer was the 'good' one among the two, and people are shown enjoying themselves and having fun.

vindication, Hogarth asked some professional witnesses (among them Thornhill) to testify, and won the case. Further proof of his abilities were found in his first major painting, 'A Scene from The Beggar's Opera' (1728), inspired from a scene of the popular John Gay farce, representing quite faithfully all the actors who had played the characters. After the success of this painting, he was asked to do others as well. This also showed Hogarth's burgeoning interest in the theatre and comic subjects.

In 1729, he eloped with Thornhill's daughter Jane. Although the marriage proved stable, the couple remained childless. Following his marriage and relative success with his book illustrations, he turned to painting small 'conversation pieces' (groups of oil portraits, 12-15 inches high). Although he initially worked fervently on these portraits, he soon tired of them, partly due to their poor remuneration. For his own enjoyment he began to record humorous events from everyday life. The painting 'Southwark Fair' (1733-34) captured a boisterous crowd during a popular festival, and showed Hogarth moving towards a new kind of 'narrative art' based on

BEER STREET.

Beer, happy Produce of our Isle
Can sinewy Strength impart,
And wearied with Fatigue and Toil
Can cheer each manly Heart

Labour and Art upheld by Thee
Successfully advance,
We quaff Thy balmy Juice with Glee
And Water leave to France

Genius of Health, thy grateful Taste
Rivals the Cup of Jove,
And warms each English generous Breast
With Liberty and Love

GIN LANE.

IPE PAWN BROKERS

GIN ROYAL

KILMAN DISTILLER

Gin cursed Fiend, with Fury fraught,
Makes human Race a Prey.
It enters by a deadly Draught,
And steals our Life away.

Virtue and Truth, driv'n to Despair,
Its Rage compells to fly,
But cherishes, with hellish Care,
Theft, Murder, Perjury.

Damn'd Cup! that on the Vitals preys,
That liquid Fire contains,
Which Madness to the Heart conveys,
And rolls it thro' the Veins.

Price 1ˢ.

contemporary city life. But it was with the story of a country girl moving to London and her consequent miseries, that showed Hogarth ridiculing the follies and viciousness of society.

In 1731, Hogarth completed the first series of his early moral works, 'A Harlot's Progress'. This collection of six scenes appeared first as paintings (unfortunately destroyed in a fire in 1755) before being published as engravings for the general public to see. It told the story of a country girl who, once she arrives in the city, turns to prostitution, and after ebduring many vicissitudes, eventually dies of venereal disease. When the engravings were published, they proved extremely popular, and from that point on, Hogarth gained sufficient financial and artistic independence to do his 'own work'. Nonetheless, 'A Harlot's Progress' had been heavily pirated when printed, and Hogarth held back the publication of his next moral series, 'A Rake's

FACING PAGE: *Gin Lane*, etching and engraving, 1751. According to Hogarth gin brought "nothing but distress, poverty and ruin." This image showing the effects of gin on the populace is simply brutal, with an alcoholic mother letting her baby fall out of her arms, bodies picked up from the streets, people fighting each other and, at the far right, a mother giving gin to her baby! Hogarth was inspired by Breughel's 'La Cuisine Maigre' and 'La Cuisine Grasse' about healthy food accompanied with lots of grease.

ABOVE: *The Gate of Calais* or *O, the Roast Beef of Old England*, oil on canvas, 1748. The title came from a popular anti-French song. A group of starving Catholics stare longingly as a side of beef is brought from the harbour to an English tavern in the port.

Vanity of youthfull Blood | Source of every Houshold Blessing, | Guest Divine to outward Viewing, | With Freedom led to
by Misuse to poison Good! | All Charms in Innocence possessing, | Abler Minister of Ruin! | And secret Chambe
man, form'd for Social Love | But turn'd to Vice, all Plagues above, | And Thou, no less of Gift divine, | Dost Thou thy friend
rest Gift of Powers above! | Foe to thy Being, Foe to Love! | Sweet Poison of Misused Wine! | And Shew thy riot

Invented, Painted, Engrav'd, & Publish'd by Wm Hogarth June ye 25. 1735. According to Act of Parlia

Progress', until he could obtain a way to protect his artist's rights (eventually a law of that nature, known as the Hogarth Act, was passed in 1735).

'A Rake's Progress' (1735), the second cautionary tale of Hogarth's moral series, told the story of a certain Tom Rakewell, son of a rich merchant, who spends all his inherited money on luxurious living, prostitution and gambling, until ending insane in Bethlem Royal Hospital. As with its predecessor, it proved incredibly popular when published as engravings. The eight original oil paintings created for this piece are in the collection of the Sir John Soane's Museum in London, where they are normally on display in one of their galleries.

Hogarth also took to painting portraits for a time, especially for middle-class sitters. Probably the most popular among his portraits was the 1745 portrait he did of actor David Garrick while playing Shakespeare's Richard III, as Hogarth got paid the generous sum of £200 for it (more than £27,000 nowadays). Let's not forget Hogarth's famously mischievous self-portrait with his sturdy pug dog, Trump, at his side with books by Shakespeare, John Milton and Jonathan Swift underneath, also done that same year.

In between these portraits, he also did the third of his moral series 'Marriage à-la-Mode', between 1743-1745, consisting of six paintings telling the miserable tragedy of an ill-calculated marriage for money. It was considered the best in his moral series by many (certainly Hogarth's artistic talents were at its zenith), mainly because the ethics of marriage were a topic of much debate at the time. Marriages of convenience usually ended badly, and many thought that love was the sounder answer. Perhaps it was because Hogarth set this series within the upper classes as opposed to his earlier series dealing with the lower classes, that critics considered it his best work (they probably identified with what was going on there).

FACING PAGE: *A Rake's Progress, Plate III*, etching and engraving, 1735. After the success of 'A Harlot's Progress', Hogarth set to tell another moral story, this time about Tom Rakewell, a young rake who has come into some fortune after the death of his miserly father. Inevitably he squanders his fortune on drinking and gambling, and visiting houses of ill-repute, as shown here. The black spots on the prostitute's faces were an indication of syphilitic sores. Hogarth's prints had been so popular that they were commonly pirated and reproduced without his permission. To protect his rights, Hogarth petitioned for a law until the Hogarth Act was passed in 1735, protecting the copyright of engravings (only those that involved original designs).

ABOVE: Detail of *A Rake's Progress, Plate VIII*, etching and engraving, 1735. Our hero's life of excess has driven him insane and he's committed to Bethlem Hospital, London's infamous mental asylum. At the time it was common among the higher classes to visit such asylums as if they were visiting the zoo, and the well-dressed ladies at the back in the far-right of the image are entertained by the bizarre antics of the inmates.

FACING PAGE: *The First Stage of Cruelty*, etching and engraving, 1751. Among the many scenes Hogarth was witness to while walking the streets of London, were the routine acts of cruelty commited upon animals and other human beings. These incidents became a series of four prints depicting the different stages in the life of a character named Tom Nero, seen here as a child being cruel to animals for fun!

Although on various occasions Hogarth tried painting historical and biblical events (which were quite popular at the time, and paid well), he had relatively little success with them, so by 1747 he returned to prints. This time the prints weren't based on a painting, but rather on an original drawing, and aimed at an unrefined public. The first of the series were the twelve prints of 'Industry and Idleness' (1747), showing the progression in the lives of two apprentices, one who is dedicated and hard-working, and another who is lazy, commits a crime and is eventually hanged for it. This series relied on the work ethics of Protestant England of the times, where hard work paid, while taking the other (some might say easier) road could lead to dreadful consequences.

The next series of prints, done in 1751, were about the ravages of alcoholism. The first titled 'Beer Street' showed some happy-go-lucky people in the streets having fun: beer was the "good" beverage. In contrast, 'Gin Lane', the other print, showed the consequences of

FIRST STAGE OF CRUELTY.

While various Scenes of sportive Woe,
The Infant Race employ,
And tortur'd Victims bleeding shew
The Tyrant in the Boy.

Behold! a Youth of gentler Heart,
To spare the Creature's pain
O take, he cries—take all my Tart,
But Tears and Tart are vain.

Learn from this fair Example—You
Whom savage Sports delight,
How Cruelty disgusts the view
While Pity charms the sight.

id by W.Hogarth   Published according to Act of Parliament Feb.1.1751.   Price

CRUELTY IN PERFECTION.

To lawfs Love when once betray'd,
  Soon Crime to Crime succeeds:
At length beguil'd to Theft, the Maid
  By her Beguiler bleeds.

Yet learn, seducing Man! nor Night,
  With all its sable Cloud,
Can screen the guilty Deed from Sight;
  Foul Murder cries aloud.

The gaping Wounds, and blood-stain'd Steel,
  Now shock his trembling Soul:
But Oh! what Pangs his Breast must feel,
  When Death his Knell shall toll.

Published according to Act of Parliament Feb. 1. 1751.

Price 1ˢ

Design'd by W.Hˢ

Design'd and Engrav'd by Willm Hogarth   Pit Ticket   Publish'd according to Act of Parliament Novr 5 1759.

severe alcoholism with scrawny, lazy and careless people, as gin was the "bad" beverage. Coincidently this image served as support for the Gin Act of 1751. The woman at the front of 'Gin Lane' (who lets her baby fall to its death), echoed what happened to Judith Dufour, a woman who strangled her baby so she could sell its clothes to buy gin, something which nowadays would be akin to the use and abuse of illegal drugs.

These prints were later followed by his 'Four Stages of Cruelty' series, depicting the cruelty on animals Hogarth had witnessed in London. In the first print he shows people being cruel to cats and dogs, in the second a coach driver being cruel to his horse, in the third the same coach driver is seen killing a woman, and in the fourth after being condemned for murder, his body is dissected by medical

Continued on page 52

FACING PAGE: *Cruelty in Perfection*, etching and engraving, 1751. Tom Nero, who has just murdered a pregnant woman, is caught in a churchyard by a group of enraged farmers. Even Tom himself is disgusted by the act he has just committed. In the last plate, after Tom is hanged at the gallows for his crimes, his body is used for medical experiments by a group of sadistic surgeons, suggesting cruelty can be found anywhere.

ABOVE: *Pit Ticket* or *The Cockpit*, etching and engraving, 1759. This scene takes place in the Royal Cockpit in Birdcage Walk, St. James Park, where a chaotic crowd are gathered to watch two cocks fight. Ironically this was dubbed a 'Royal Sport' and we can see the many different social classes at attendance in this cruel gambling (rather than sporting) event.

THESE PAGES: *Before* and *After*, oil on canvas, 1731. These two paintings were commissioned "at the request of a certain vicious nobleman," according to Hogarth. A comical view into a romantic conquest that doesn't end up being so romantic. These paintings also became a popular set of prints in 1736.

THESE PAGES: *Marriage-à-la-Mode, The Lady's Death*, oil on canvas, 1743-1745. This was part of a series of six paintings (this being the second one) centred around a marriage for profit. Many consider these to be Hogarth's best work, and indeed he shines as a skilled painter here, filling in every inch of the canvas with detail.

THESE PAGES: *David Garrick as Richard III,* oil on canvas, 1745. Garrick (1717-1779) was a hugely influential actor (and stage manager) of the day. In this painting we see him as Richard III in his tent just before the Battle of Bosworth, haunted by the ghosts of those he has murdered. However, this scene didn't play as Hogarth showed it, all coming instead from his imagination. Hogarth also received a huge amount for the painting, £200, which at the time was the largest sum ever paid for a painting. Art critics consider this painting to be more than a simple portrait, linking it as being historical too, although based on a play.

Continued from page 45

scientists. This last part reflecting the 1752 Act of Parliament, in the name of science, allowing for the dissection of criminals who had been executed for murder.

Between those years, Hogarth organised various auctions of his paintings, although they sold for extremely low prices. Dissatisfied, he took to isolation, although he would continue to produce prints, mainly as a reflection of his own ideas. His 'Election' series, done between 1754-1758, tried to bring back his humour and sardonic point of view, in a series of crowded and very elaborate canvasses. But interest in his work had been waning, even after he himself was appointed serjeant painter to King George III.

During his last years, Hogarth suffered from ill-health, mainly due to the lack of interest from the public in his work. The fact that one of his historical paintings, 'Sigismunda Mourning over the Heart of Guiscardo' (1759) had been rejected by his patron, didn't help his general state of mind either. Nevertheless, Hogarth, ever the sardonic satirist, still managed to deliver, although his anti-war satire in 'The Times, Plate I' brought public outrage. Supposedly the first in a series of two, these engravings contained some of Hogarth's most pessimistic views on the political machinations and corruptions of the day. The second plate, in fact, was suppressed by Hogarth himself, and then by his widow, and wasn't published until 1790.

FACING PAGE: *The Times, Plate I*, etching and engraving, 1762. A series of two prints, only the first appeared during Hogarth's lifetime. In this elaborate political allegory (each building representing a different country at war), Hogarth idealised and defended King George III and the Earl of Bute's ministry and attacked their enemies. However, this didn't sit well with critics or the public who were tired of wars, so Hogarth shelved the second print (which was a resolution to what is shown here) and it wasn't printed until 1790—after the death of both Hogarth and his widow.

The Times
Plate I

Published as the Act Directs
Sepr. 7 1762

53

ABOVE: *Tailpiece* or *The Bathos*, etching and engraving, 1764. Hogarth's paintings and engravings were more or less a series of stories told in pictures. Here, showing the last work he produced depicting the Apocalypse without an afterlife, we find a slightly surreal (before the term was ever coined) image by Hogarth. Has the main figure, the Angel of Death (some believe it was Hogarth himself, notice a print of his 'The Times' at the figure's feet), finally given up all hope and destroyed the world? Notice the cloud of smoke coming from his mouth forming the word "Finis" ("The End"), a staple that would later be used in comic books as word balloons when the characters speak. In Italy word balloons are referred to as 'fumetti' (puffs of smoke). Could Hogarth's prints have been the precursors to today's comic strips and graphic novels?

Although pretty much dissatisfied with everything, Hogarth worked diligently almost until his last dying days, completing the sardonically titled 'Tailpiece', or 'The Bathos' a few months before his death. In this piece he depicted the demise of a person (the artist?) as both an angel and a demon, with a cloud forming out of his mouth with the word 'Finis' written inside it. Could this had been a precursor to comic books, with text within a cloud forming out of a person's mouth? Yet, Hogarth's paintings as a series of tableaus telling a story could also be the framework for a movie (or the equivalent of the storyboards).

Hogarth died on October 26, 1764. Yet, his influence has been massive throughout the centuries, among writers, comedians and filmmakers, and also among the cartoonists from *Punch*, the "usual gang of idiots" at *MAD*, and all the way to underground cartoonists such as Robert Crumb, perhaps the modern successor to Hogarth. ●

IN THE NEXT ISSUE

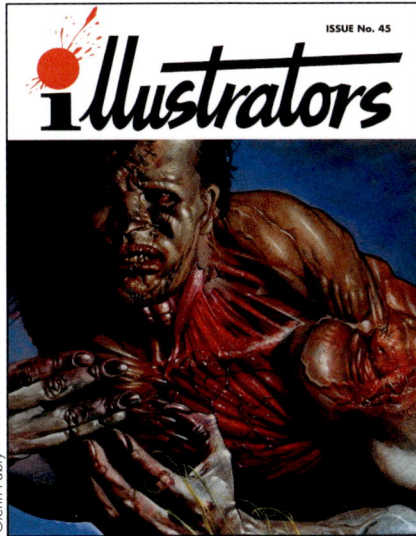

ISSUE No. 45

Glenn Fabry

Glenn Fabry

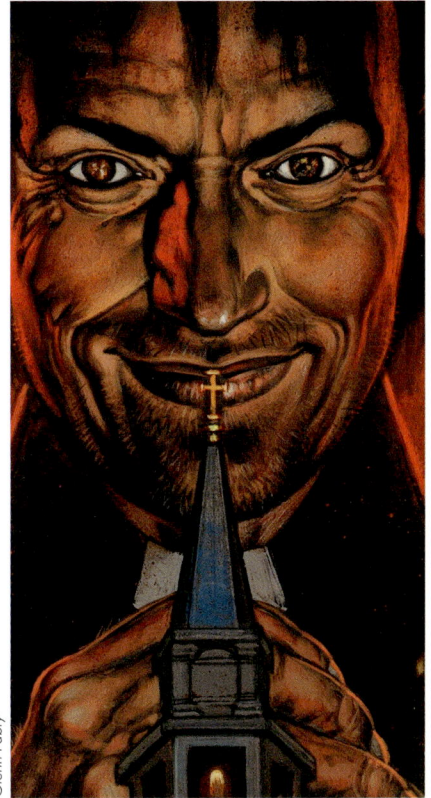

Glenn Fabry

We open with Glenn Fabry who became one of the seminal artists from 2000AD in the UK, and then went on to become one of the favourite cover illustrators from the Vertigo line of comics in the USA.

Then we remember Glen (with only one 'N') Orbik who brought back all the thrills and chills from the crime pulp covers of the 1940s into the new millennium. We take a look back at Howard Chandler Christy creator of the Christy Girl, and at some German children's books about children behaving badly and how they inspired some popular comic strips and animated cartoons.

Glen Orbik

Howard Chandler Christy

Wilhelm Busch

Photo by Jack Woodhams

Murugiah

FACING PAGE: Detail from *Styx*, **digital, 2020.**
ABOVE: The artist himself at his studio about to get a surprise visit from us.

We visit the strange and weird psilocybin sugar-coated multi-inter-dimensional universe of this artist who seems to have landed from a different and colourful planet, and attempt to find out what he is all about with our recent chat.

As AN AWARD-WINNING ARTIST, MURUGIAH has specialised in illustration, typography and design. A multi-talented artist who draws inspiration from his Sri Lankan heritage, even though he was born in England, raised in Wales and lives nowadays in London. He discovered art as young lad reading comics and watching cartoons and movies, but trained in architecture before finally deciding that art was his true calling. He has been self-taught ever since, searching for his own, immediately recognisable art style.

His illustrations are mostly from the psychedelic realm, inspired by Eastern mysticism, and on a recent trip to Mexico, found another source of inspiration that he hopes to put to use in the future. He has worked with such diverse clients as Disney, Marvel, Wired and Mondo, to name but a few. He has recently turned to sculpture and fine art. Lastly, he considers himself "a candy-coated psilocybin particle bean daydreamer."

I met him during one rainy London afternoon and we talked about his favourite subject, drawing!

IQ: Your work would fit perfectly during the psychedelic 1960s, yet you weren't even born then…
M: Yes, I've been told that it reminds people of the 'Yellow Submarine' movie, but I wasn't even aware of that when I began working in my style.

IQ: How did you get interested in drawing? Was it something you saw and wished you could do the same? What artists inspired you?

M: Well, I never really saw drawings that inspired me. It was pretty much films, TV shows and comic books. The comic books really must have inspired me to draw… But I preferred time alone, time to myself. I spent a lot of time in my room, and I must have picked up pencil and paper and started drawing things… But I thank my art classes and my art teacher at school—obviously we were drawing in art class—and I must have shown a real enjoyment for the drawing. I think I must be autistic because when drawing something I forget about everything else. I think it was a combination of drawing in my art classes in school and watching cartoons, like X-Men, in the 1990s. But very specifically, I can't remember when I began drawing.

IQ: You mentioned comic books, what comics did you read?

M: I was reading *Spider-Man* and *X-Men* comics as a child, and as an adult now I have a very different love of comics. I'm currently reading a comic called *Rare Flavours*. I don't know if you're familiar with it?

IQ: No… Well, actually I stopped reading comics a long time ago.

M: Oh, all right. This one is based on someone like Anthony Beaurdine who likes travel and food. So it's very, very different. But as a child, I very much read the superhero stuff. That's what got me into comics, cartoons and Saturday mornings.

IQ: Did you ever thought of doing comics yourself?

M: It's something that never entered my mind, because I'm more of a visual person, less of a story person. So I would enjoy the big splash pages… very specific panels from comic books. The same in movies, I watch them and focus more on the big, grandiose image… like in 'Terminator 2' and the first 'Terminator', both of those films open with a vision of the future where the exoskeletons have taken over, and their big armies and the fighting. Those were the things I tend to concentrate on more. The same thing with my images today, one image tells a lot of stuff, rather than sequential things. So I mainly concentrate on telling a story with one image, rather than, you know, sequential story-telling…

ABOVE: *AR*, digital, 2020.

FACING PAGE: *Elton John*, screen print commemorating his 75 years, digital, 2022. Commissioned by Collectionzz for Elton John.

Elton John

COMMEMORATING ★★★ 75 YEARS

ABOVE: *Lake Shore Night Drive II*, giclée with metallic gold acrylic Screen Print embellishments, 2021.

IQ: There's so much detail in your images that I wonder whether you were inspired by Japanese animation. More specifically the work of Satoshi Kon. There's so much detail on every frame of his films, that I wonder, uh—do you actually know his work?

M: I came to the work of Satoshi Kon later. Maybe when I was 17, 18, 19 years old. I guess I grew up with the very American Disney influence, and then I started watching films like 'Perfect Blue', 'Paprika', 'Akira' and 'Memories'. Yeah, so things like that, I started watching a bit later on. So they must have had an influence on some level. Yes. And I still watch those movies today. I

love them so much.

IQ: *Looking at your work, I don't think of Disney. I'm thinking more of Oriental stuff, so I thought you must have watched a lot of Japanese animation.*

M: Well, I watch a lot of Japanese animation now, and it probably has an influence on what I do now. As you say, the busyness, the complication of the images, rather than any specific details, might come from that. I really enjoy those films now, but not when I was younger.

IQ: *I also see you've done some posters for movies, concerts… Were those commissions?*

M: The posters were commissioned by film studios, or Mondo. I don't remember if you did the interview with Jason Edmiston (*yes—Ed.*), but he also did commissions for film studios and Mondo, and that's what I do, too. They are officially licensed, and you get permission from the film studios and the directors, although there are a couple of private commissions where I don't have an approval from the film studios, but it's private, so it's OK. Most of them are officially licensed.

IQ: *So you are also part of the Mondo team, more or less?*

M: More or less… yes. I started making posters for them in 2019, not that long ago, and I made 11 posters from then until now, with the old art directing team. Sadly,

that art directing team was let go when they were taken over by Funko Pop! And now I don't want to work with that company anymore because they fired these amazing art directors that showed a passion for me. I'm looking forward to working with those same art directors in whatever they do in the future. Most of the original Mondo artists are done with Mondo. I can't speak for all of them, but most don't want to work with them anymore. We had a good time, a good run. I was one of the last people who worked for these fine art directors.

IQ: Do you also design toys?

M: Not so much toys, as sculptures that I design, as with this one (*shows the sculpture in question, done in resin and standing on a small round marble platform–Ed.*) which is a representation of me. His name is Muru. That's my avatar. It's a resin sculpture, and I've got another here, slightly larger one (*shows the other one–Ed.*), but what I like doing is more in line with the sculpture art of people I studied, like Henry Moore and Barbara Hepworth. Using natural material like stone and wood. I'm trying to create my sculptures in a similar way, using that raw material instead of colourful ones as in toys. I think it's a new way of expressing my work in sculptural form. In painting and digital form, it's quite colourful, so I want to

see how I can represent my artwork in a very natural sculpture form.

IQ: Are the sculptures you just showed me done by hand?

M: They are 3D modelled and we get them printed basically. I realise as I've become busier and busier with work, I just want to focus on the thing I love the most, which is drawing and painting. And if I can delegate as much as possible, I choose to.

IQ: Let's get back to your artwork. Was the Mondo work done digitally?

M: What I do for Mondo was done digitally, yes. Most of the time it starts out as a very loose sketch, where I'm coming up with the basic forms and shapes. I have an

FACING PAGE: Mural at the Picturehouse Cinema in Chester, 2023. The mural was unveiled by the Lord Mayor of Chester, Cllr Sheila Little, when she opened the building on November 8, 2023.

ABOVE: R*angoli Mirrored Cosmos***, public art sculpture, 2023. Located at Greenwich Peninsula in London.**

example here (*shows a notepad with a sketch done in red biro–Ed.*). This is a sketch for a 'Dune' poster. I was commissioned by Mondo and Warner Bros. to do a poster of 'Dune'. I knew immediately I wanted to include a giant eye, the sand-worm coming in and out of the poster, and I wanted the letters of Dune to be split on all four corners of the poster. So I much more think in these large compositional forms and then I go straight into digital and start refining and refining until I get to the poster I want. It is very similar to sculpture, you start with this large clump of clay and you start refining and refining until you get your form, where as here I'm starting with this very loose sketch and I'm slowly, slowly refining it.

It's not the same way with my fine artwork. For that I have a drawing on paper, a sketch, which I refine by hand, then I recreate on canvas or trace it onto a nice watercolour paper, and paint and draw from there. Here, let me show you (*pulls up a painting on a circular canvas–Ed.*). This was done on paper first, refining the sketch and then projecting it onto the canvas with a projector—
IQ: Excuse me, but where did you get a round canvas?
M: (*Laughs*) My friend gave it to me for my birthday. She was so impressed with what I did with it, on that circular

FACING PAGE: *Cried a River and Drowned the Whole World,* acrylics on canvas, 2022.

canvas. You can get them at art shops, so they aren't too hard to find.

As I was saying, the drawing ends up on the blank canvas, and as you are refining the painting you adapt the line, so it's really a nice process, because I'm not starting from scratch on the canvas creating a very loose line work. The projector goes away and then I'm refining the lines and doing all kind of paint effects, like drip paint effects and background textures. I'm adapting as I go. I'm not starting with this very refined sketch, I'm adapting from it until the final form which ends up being something different from what I had started with. And it's different from… Well, it's kind of similar to the way I work digitally.

BELOW: *Masquerade,* digital, 2020.

WARNER BROS. PICTURES AND LEGENDARY PICTURES PRESENT A LEGENDARY PICTURES PRODUCTION A FILM BY DENIS VILLENEUVE "DUNE" TIMOTHÉE CHALAMET REBECCA FERGUSON OSCAR ISAAC JOSH BROLIN STELLAN SKARSGÅRD DAVE BAUTISTA STEPHEN McKINLEY HENDERSON ZENDAYA CHANG CHEN with CHARLOTTE RAMPLING with JASON MOMOA and JAVIER BARDEM MUSIC BY HANS ZIMMER TANYA LAPOINTE JOSHUA GRODE HERBERT W. GAINS JON SPAIHTS THOMAS TULL BRIAN HERBERT BYRON MERRITT KIM HERBERT MARY PARENT, p.g.a. DENIS VILLENEUVE, p.g.a. CALE BOYTER, p.g.a. JOE CARACCIOLO, J. BASED ON THE NOVEL "DUNE" WRITTEN BY FRANK HERBERT SCREENPLAY BY JON SPAIHTS AND DENIS VILLENEUVE AND ERIC ROTH DIRECTED BY DENIS VILLENEUVE

FACING PAGE: *Dissociation*, acrylics on paper, 2023.

LEFT: *Dune*, digital, 2022. Commissioned by Mondo and Warner Bros.

FOLLOWING PAGES LEFT: *WandaVision*, digital, 2022. Commissioned by Mondo and Marvel.

FOLLOWING PAGES RIGHT: *Doctor Strange in the Multiverse of Madness*, digital, 2022. As a child Murugiah loved superhero comics and cartoons. Getting a chance to draw his favourite superheroes commissioned by Mondo and Marvel was a pleasant surprise.

IQ: *What do you use for your paintings? Acrylics?*
M: Mainly acrylics, because I tend to use a background texture which is very wet, and create these drip effects, and once that's dry, I'll use very clean, flat acrylics, to almost recreate the same way I do digitally, but on a canvas. It will never be a true recreation of the digital work, because the painting is thick, the canvas has a different texture… I like the differences of the material.

IQ: *You work mostly with flat colours…*
M: Yes. Yeah… I think it is to me a good way to make the images bold, bright and recognisable as my style. I haven't got into shading those colours yet. Maybe it's something I might do in the future, but at the moment I work in this identifiable style that suits me and my inspiration, and the influence from the TV shows I mentioned, the cartoons. So, yeah, it's bright and positive and sunny, although there might be some dark stuff in

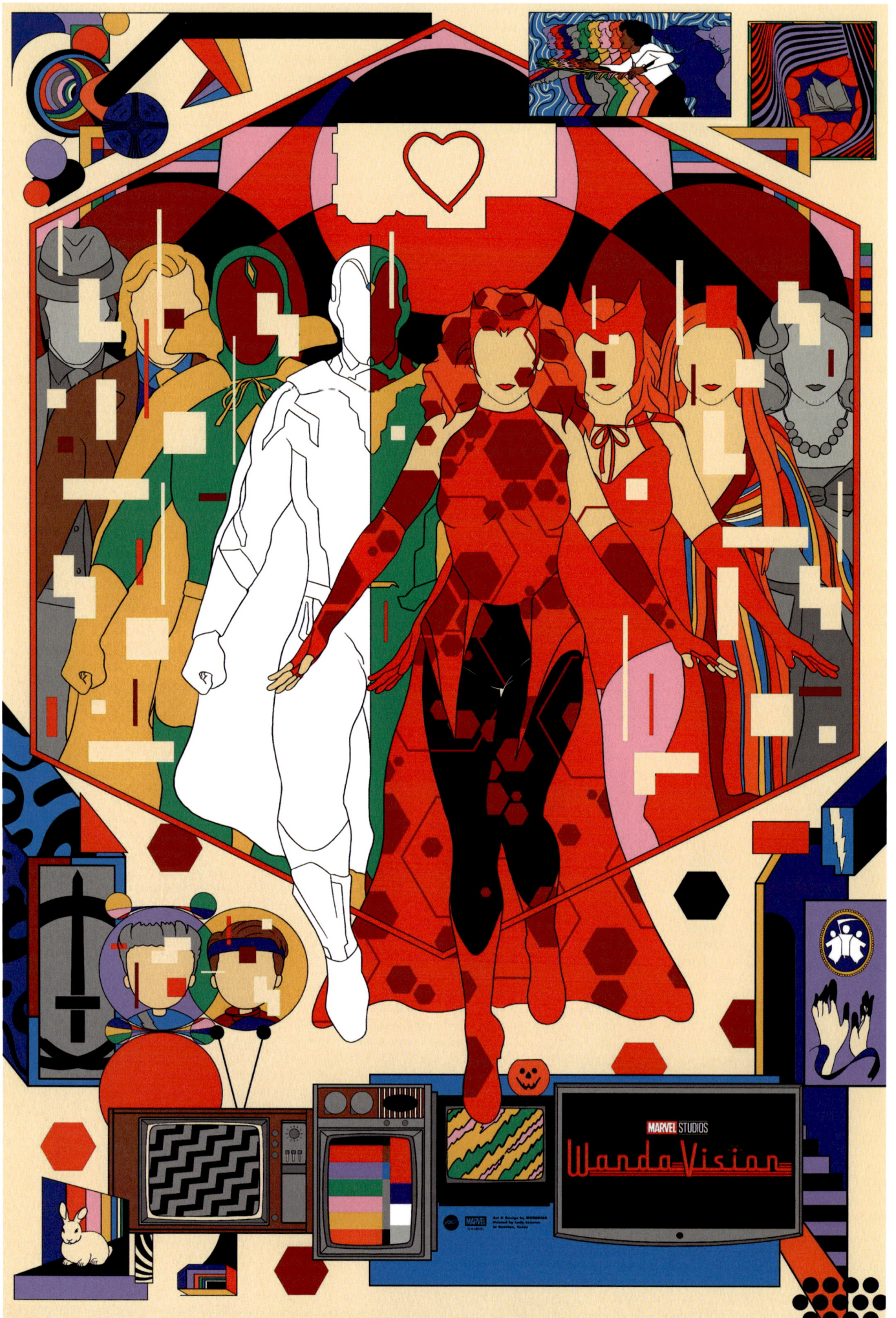

MARVEL STUDIOS
WandaVision

MARVEL STUDIOS

DOCTOR STRANGE
IN THE
MULTIVERSE OF MADNESS

MARVEL STUDIOS PRESENTS A KEVIN FEIGE PRODUCTION BENEDICT CUMBERBATCH
"DOCTOR STRANGE IN THE MULTIVERSE OF MADNESS" ELIZABETH OLSEN CHIWETEL EJIOFOR BENEDICT WONG XOCHITL GOMEZ WITH MICHAEL STÜHLBARG AND RACHEL McADAMS CASTING BY SARAH HALLEY FINN, CSA
MUSIC SUPERVISOR DAVE JORDAN MUSIC BY DANNY ELFMAN VISUAL EFFECTS PRODUCER IAN JOYNER VISUAL EFFECTS SUPERVISOR JANEK SIRRS VISUAL EFFECTS AND ANIMATION BY INDUSTRIAL LIGHT & MAGIC COSTUME DESIGNER GRAHAM CHURCHYARD EDITED BY BOB MURAWSKI, ACE TIA NOLAN, ACE
PRODUCTION DESIGNER CHARLES WOOD DIRECTOR OF PHOTOGRAPHY JOHN MATHIESON, BSC PRODUCERS MITCH BELL RICHIE PALMER EXECUTIVE PRODUCERS VICTORIA ALONSO ERIC HAUSERMAN CARROLL SCOTT DERRICKSON JAMIE CHRISTOPHER
EXECUTIVE PRODUCER LOUIS D'ESPOSITO PRODUCED BY KEVIN FEIGE, p.g.a. WRITTEN BY MICHAEL WALDRON DIRECTED BY SAM RAIMI

MONTREUX JAZZ FESTIVAL 2021

RESTART

NEW FOUND GLORY

MAKE THE MOST OF IT ACOUSTIC TOUR • 2023

THE TOWN HALL • NEW YORK • MARCH 18 • 2023

Continued from page 67

the background, with darker meanings. But, yes, very bold and bright is what I go for.

IQ: Digitally, what do you use? Photoshop?

M: I use Photoshop for the digital work and clean up any drawings, and that's it. I don't use anything else.

IQ: When did you start working digitally? Back in my day personal computers didn't exist, so you had to draw everything by hand.

M: (*Laughs*) I started using digital tools in my final year in school. It was very basic, very rudimentary. My art teacher always told me that it was a tool to use, rather than an end product. Which is why I don't like things like Procreate where an entire image is created on an iPad and there's no transfer of the image to canvas or to paper or scanning texture. None of that exists. It's all done in one place. I started using Photoshop when I was 19, but I dropped it when I studied architecture, because I didn't use it as much there. And then when I quit architecture and transitioned into being an artist, I picked up Photoshop again. But I use it as a tool rather than a primary source.

I like to get away from the computer as much as possible. Either project the image onto canvas or paper, just to get away from spending so much time in front of a screen. It's really important to get off the screen. I recently came back from a three and a half weeks holiday in Mexico, and it helped me realise that there's more to life than staring at a screen.

PREVIOUS PAGES LEFT: *Montreux Jazz Festival 2021*, digital, 2021. Probably the most famous music festival in Europe, they hold an annual contest to find the best poster for their annual festival. This was Murugiah's proposition. It was long listed among the final 30.

PREVIOUS PAGES RIGHT: *New Found Glory*, digital, 2023. A four-colour screen print commissioned by New Found Glory's Make the Most of It Acoustic tour show at the Town Hall, New York City in 2023.

THIS PAGE: *Muru*, digital model and sculpture, 2022.

FACING PAGE: *Heavy Metal*, digital, 2023. Proposed cover for the once popular science-fantasy magazine that unfortunately closed its doors in July 2023. This cover sadly never got to be printed.

COMPASSION

MURUGIAH

IQ: Speaking of Mexico, I see some of Mexico in your work. Maybe not the folklore per se, but the use of colours and mysticism. Back in my youth it was a very colourful country, you'd see all these bright colours on the buildings, each with different colours.

M: Well, Mexico City is pretty grey, similar to London, but when you go to Oaxaca, San Cristobal, Mérida, all the buildings are very bright and colourful, and the artwork is very mystical and folkloric. I got a lot of inspiration coming from Mexico. My future work will be even more Mexican, I think (*laughs*).

IQ: Speaking of which, I also see the influence of Moebius and Jodorowsky on your work. Were they a source of inspiration somehow?

M: Yes. I named one of my cats Moebius. Maybe five years ago, a friend took me to a double feature of 'El Topo' and 'The Holy Mountain'. This was right before I started all of this work, she took me to see this double-feature, and my mind was changed forever. I wanted to make work on mysticism… on psychedelia…

I was very interested on Moebius, and I did a lot of research on him. He was so influential on all the movies that I liked, films like 'Alien', 'Dune', 'The Fifth Element', 'Tron'—Moebius was the artist behind all of those things. And I've collected a lot of Moebius art, as well.

And Jodorowsky's meaning behind his films, what he's interested in, goes very well with what I'm interested in: the mysticism, the tarot…

They are probably the most influential, even if you don't see it directly, they are the most influential on my work. I never got to meet Moebius, and Jodorowsky… Well, what's he now? Like 90-something. He's an old guy…

FACING PAGE: *Compassion*, digital, 2023.

BELOW: *Choose Love*, window installation, 2023. Part of the 'Compassion' project commissioned by the Southbank Centre for the Royal Festival Hall in London.

the ultimate trip

IQ: *He's still as sharp as ever, and if he could he'd still be making movies. I mean, if he could raise the money that is. He said he wanted to live past one hundred. Otherwise he writes scripts mainly for comic books. The only thing is that if you ever meet him, the first thing he wants to do is read you the tarot. If you believe in that, there's no problem. Otherwise…*

Anyway, there's huge influence from Asian culture in your paintings. Your parents are from Sri Lanka, have you been there?

M: I have been to Sri Lanka but when I was very young. My plan is to make work like a Westerner looking into Sri Lanka. Then when I get to go there in a few years time, I think the work will start to change and become more South-Asian inspired, but at the moment it's going from the West to the East. So maybe it will go the other way round after that..

IQ: *Did you see or have any art books at home while growing up that might have inspired you?*

M: No, that came from my art teacher, who was this Polish guy. He would just give us an art book or show us Antoni Gaudi and say, "Start making something like this." Or show us Hieronymus Bosch's work and say, "Show me something like this." We would do that in art classes and he would go to his corner and start cutting lino. His wife was the librarian at school, and she would say that he would always be cutting the lino in bed. They'd be sleeping next to each other, and he'd be cutting the lino on bed, with lino shavings everywhere. He was a very eccentric, fun man. He taught me everything I know about art. The more fine art… I still have some of the books he gave me on my shelf, from all those years ago. I need to call him and thank him for all he has done for me.

IQ: *Were you the one who showed the most interest in art?*

M: I was one of the two. There were two or three students that really showed a lot of interest. But by the time we were 18, I was probably the one who showed the most interest, and that's why he gravitated towards me. I think he knew that I was going to be an artist.

IQ: *You were studying architecture when you decided to become an artist. Did you go to art school?*

FACING PAGE LEFT: A *Clockwork Orange*, digital, 2020. Commissioned by Mondo with the Kubrick Estate.

FACING PAGE RIGHT: *2001 A Space Odyssey*, digital, 2020. Commissioned by Mondo with the Kubrick Estate. Murugiah is hoping to continue his work on Kubrick's oeuvre.

M: I just started drawing and learning from there. I had already spent so much time training as an architect that I thought I should just get started and get on with it. I quit architecture in 2012 and I discovered this new style I work in today in 2019. It took a long time to get to where I am.

I like to work slowly, that's the way I work. So it makes sense that it took this long for my art to develop.

IQ: *Any projects you are working on now?*
M: Yes, I'll have an art show for the end of next year. So I'll be spending a year building a body of work on canvas and paper, which I'm very excited about. And then, along with a group of collaborators I've worked with in

the past, we are going to see about pitching a project we can do for Summer next year.

So now, we've come to the end of the year where I branded a musical festival, I've had a public art sculpture, a big charity collaboration, and that's it for this year. I only have one private film poster I'm doing right now, and then I'm going to start working on my art show. ●

● *You can visit Murugiah's webpage:* **www.murugiah.com**. *He's also present on instagram and twitter.*

ABOVE: *Garden Party,* **digital, 2022.**

Illustrators back issues and Specials!

Get your copies while you can! Some issues are already sold out!
Low stock and very few copies on others! Hurry, copies are limited!

 **Special 17** Trigan Empire Artists

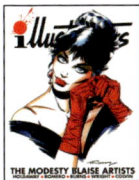 **Special 16** The Modesty Blaise Artists

 **Special 15** The Art of Tarzan

 **Special 14** History of Warren Mags

 **Special 13** The Art of Glamour

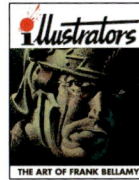 **Special 11** The Art of Frank Bellamy

 **Special 10** Sydney Jordan/ Jim Holdaway

 **Special 9** Crime Comics

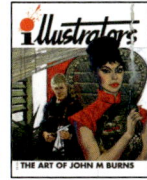 **Special 8** The Art of John Burns

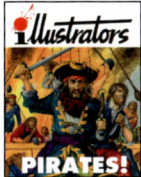 **Special 7** Pirates!

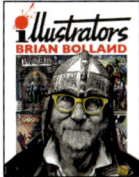 **Special 6** The Art of Brian Bolland

 **Special 5** The Art of Commando

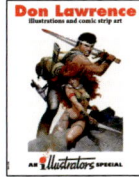 **Special 3** Don Lawrence Illustrations

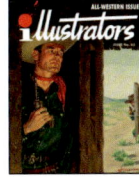 **Issue 43**

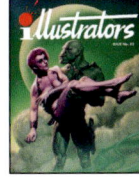 **Issue 42**

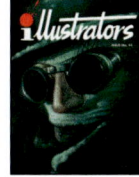 **Issue 41**

 **Issue 40**

 **Issue 39**

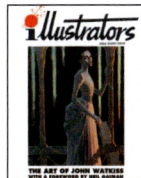 **Issue 38**

 **Issue 37**

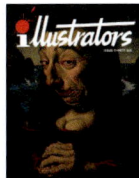 **Issue 36**

 **Issue 35**

 **Issue 34**

 **Issue 33**

 **Issue 32**

 **Issue 31**

 **Issue 30**

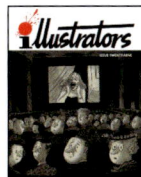 **Issue 29**

 **Issue 28**

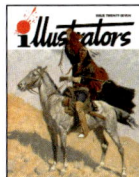 **Issue 27**

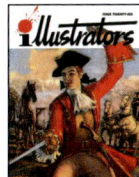 **Issue 26**

 **Issue 25**

 **Issue 24**

 **Issue 23**

 **Issue 22** (Low stock)

 **Issue 21**

 **Issue 20**

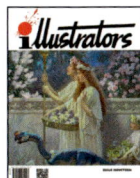 **Issue 19** (Low stock)

 **Issue 18**

 **Issue 17**

 **Issue 16**

 **Issue 15**

 **Issue 14**

 **Issue 13**

 **Issue 12** (Low stock)

 **Issue 11**

 **Issue 10**

 **Issue 9**

 **Issue 8**

 **Issue 7**

 **Issue 6**

 **Issue 5**

 **Issue 4**

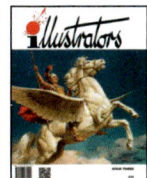 **Issue 3**

To AI or not to AI

AI is taking control of our lives in ways which are not immediately apparent. Anyone can now create art without any artistic knowledge or being able to hold a pencil or a brush. Should we rejoice at this or start to worry? Fear not, as Diego Cordoba decides to explore the world of AI.

HAVE A MONKEY HIT KEYS RANDOMLY ON A TYPEWRITER OR COMPUTER KEYBOARD for an infinite amount of time and he'll end up writing something, even the complete works of Shakespeare. Apparently with AI you too could become the next Frazetta or Norman Rockwell. But how true is this, and do illustrators need to worry and should publishers rejoice at not needing to hire anyone to create illustrations?

Back when personal computers first became available, many thought they would take over from artists. Just by pressing keys on the keyboard a finished image would appear. However, computers are nothing more that a tool, just as a pen, a pencil or a brush, and artists used them as such. A person had to create that image manipulating a computer. The difference between digital and hand-painted art being that for the latter you have a physical original piece of work as opposed to a virtual one. Nonetheless, since illustrations generally appear as printed matter, won't it be the same whether it is done digitally or by hand?

The fact that digital art has been used all throughout the world, lead us to

All images randomly created using different AI generators. Should real illustrators begin to worry?

BELOW LEFT: *Barbarian duck and pretty damsel in distress*, AI rendition. "This was the first illustration I did using an AI generator. I wanted to get creative and surrealistic, and asked for a barbarian duck and this is what I got."

BELOW RIGHT: *A girl being attacked by a bug-eyed monster in outer space*, AI rendition. "First sci-fi image I asked for, however the AI generator took the word 'girl' too literally as opposed to what I had in mind. Also, the girl looks like a character from a CG-animation film. On a different AI platform I later demanded a 'beautiful woman' instead and got the version on the facing page."

FACING PAGE TOP: *Beautiful woman being attacked by a bug-eyed monster inside a spaceship*, AI rendition. "Does this look as if the monster is attacking the beautiful woman? How are we supposed to know she's beautiful when she's seen from behind and at a small size? Where are the bug-eyes on the monster? Why does the 'bug-eyed' monster look like a generic monster created for a Hollywood CGI-enhanced movie?"

LEFT: *A girl laughing at a bug-eyed alien from outer space,* AI rendition. "Since all the AI images seemed expressionless (see following page), I decided to go for extremes and had the girl laughing, although the alien found this hilarious as well. For some reason all human figures in this platform ended up looking Asian. While the artwork shown here may seem competent enough, the whole setting seems unrelated, and any bodily position, besides standing up, seems impossible to create. AI takes the words literally when you say you want your figures to fold their arms or sit with their legs crossed. Other bodily functions such as picking your nose or scratching your ear, waving, punching, running, etc., seem impossible to render. Not to mention that the artwork rendered with AI comes out uniformly and in one singular graphic style, making all the images look generic."

ABOVE LEFT: *Woman combing her hair in front of a mirror*, AI rendition. "This time I wanted a photographic-look. Why she come out looking Asian, I don't know (see previous page). The face is completely expressionless, although I didn't ask for her to be smiling or laughing—but who does that while combing their hair? And although the image might be close to a photograph, it also feels unnatural and eerie the way she stares blankly at the mirror while combing her hair. Overall the figure seems to come from a software used for 3D modelling."

ABOVE RIGHT: *Cowboy riding his horse and being pursued by Indians over the desert*, AI rendition. "The Indians seem to have gone out for a stroll. Not much action going on here, which AI seems to avoid or not be able to accomplish any movement besides simply standing. The legs of some horses look wonky, AI not being able to understand the movement of a horse's legs (which by the way, is extremely hard to draw or paint even by hand). Although it might not be clear here (the image being so small) some horses are missing parts of their body, one not even having a head. From afar the image looks fine, until you get closer and notice all the mistakes. All the characters look stiff and with no emotion."

believe it really doesn't matter what you use to create your artwork. On the other hand, we now have something called 'Artificial Intelligence'. What exactly is this, and should artists start to worry about it?

I decided to try out AI myself, and it really requires no artistic knowledge or creativity on your part. You simply type in what you would like to see, and the AI generator will render what you wrote as an image. You can even choose between different artistic styles—from surreal to photorealistic, painterly or 3D rendering—size, format and setting. But is it any good, you ask?

The images rendered come from a rather large image database. Once you type in what you want, AI will randomly choose images corresponding to the words you typed in, and build a composite picture. The results can be surprising in more ways than one. I noticed that the more complicated you want your image to be, the harder it is for the AI generator to fully comprehend all what you want (my first attempt for a barbarian duck came out as utter nonsense). It has a hard time rendering action scenes as all images are rather static and movement of any sort comes out wonky or missing parts. Add to this the fact that even though there are many ways and styles to choose from to render the image, all are similar or as if generated from a 3D modelling software used in video games. Painting styles in AI come from images harvested from the public domain, however, there are copyright issues on many that still have been sourced from creators without permission. This may include comic book and cartoon characters, and certain well-known illustrators. As to book publishers wanting to use AI instead of an illustrator, well, the generator doesn't understand more than a sentence, and the monkey who wrote all of Shakespeare's work has more chances of becoming then next Frazetta than an AI generator.

In conclusion AI, as it currently stands, is far from a rival to artistic expression. Whether artists can successfully integrate it into their work flow is debatable—but it is here to stay. For better or worse. ●

Create your own AI illustrations

We asked some of our collaborators to create their own illustrations with AI, and share with us their experience.

Peter Richardson, Editor

Saint Greta

"I did want Greta to look more Holbeinesque but with a smidge of encephalopathy thrown in. However, still unnervingly good!"

Norman Boyd, Collaborator

Thunderbirds by Mike Noble

"I chose to follow Peter and looked at Greta 'drawn by Roy Lichtenstein', and then played with the filters on the AI generator, but the results were pretty bad really. I tried the same in other AI platforms, and again, was not worried about illustrators' careers! I then read a wonderful article on researchers trying to grasp what the underlying materials AI are using and they discovered that many pieces on the training database are well known artworks or photographs!

"I then tried asking for 'Thunderbirds' in different styles, which shows that this comic copyright work is not on their database. Even worse, the aeroplanes just seem to be pieced together haphazardly, with their wings attached wherever. None of them would ever fly in the real world!"

Renaissance Lady laughing and picking her nose

"At first glance, the result seemed fine, in an eerie sort of way, including the woman's maniacal laughter. However, the weirdest aspect of this Renaissance painting was the lady holding what seems to be a human nose in one hand with a toothpick stuck to it! She also has six fingers on her left hand (yes, count them), that I never asked for.

"AI works fine if all you want is a portrait of a friend or a loved one, as you can upload a photo and turn it into a painting. However, keep what you ask for simple, and don't use complicated words or words that may have different meanings. The results can be hilarious, but useless for publication.

"As a fun source to create weird pictures, this can be great, but, again, not for professional use. There's a glitch in the matrix with the meaning of words and rendering of some images."

Dylan Hervais-Adleman, Manager of subscriptions and distribution

An Orchestra of drunken crab sheriffs on horseback defeating a band of marauding politicians

"In short, I like the image and would like it printed on a t-shirt, or possibly framed in my kid's bedroom to help give them imaginative dreams. However, I do not understand where the band of marauding politicians are, I don't understand why the odd flag things are so Dali-esque (or what they are)... I don't understand why the protagonist crab sheriff is furry or why the horses have long shaved donkey-ears (and in some cases, disfigured twisted plasticine heads)... I don't understand why there is so much sky-borne activity, I don't understand why my Crab sheriffs have so few legs and so few claws... or why they aren't wearing star badges—are they off duty?

"I do very much like the atmosphere and the subtleties in this piece, but it seems that many of the prompts have been mismanaged or misinterpreted by the model."

As a publisher, Mr. West opted for what every publisher dreams of having: an AI that can replicate the work of the Great Masters of Illustration (and not having to pay them). Here were his results:

Mona Lisa in the style of Frank Frazetta
"Huh?"

British MPs fighting Crusaders
"Apparently the AI generator didn't get the joke. Why are some Crusaders riding backwards on their horses?"

Mona Lisa in the style of Frank Bellamy
"Huh?"

Robin Hood by Robert Crumb
"Robin's Merry Men in the background are riding backwards. Maybe they are a tad too merry?"

"I tried 'Dick Turpin by Jim Holdaway' and 'Dick Turpin by Robert Crumb', but both images violated the AI community guidelines. I guess it doesn't like the word Dick."

Problems with AI generators

Although many may believe they can become illustrators thanks to AI, the generator itself poses some serious problems.

ALTHOUGH AI MIGHT BE SOMETHING amusing to play around with in your spare time, it does pose some serious problems. And it's not because it will replace actual illustrators (as you might have seen with the examples shown in the previous pages, it's far from doing so). The main problem is with copyright infringement. Yes, AI is a generator that has to learn how to create images and to do so it relies on an image database. To fill that database you have to load or scan images the generator will later use to create new ones. Unfortunately some artwork is owned by its original creators and have a copyright. Any artwork that isn't in the public domain can't be reproduced in any form or way without consent from its rightful owner.

The next problem with AI is that it doesn't know how to draw, it only relies on the large stock of images in its database. The generator doesn't know wrong from right or what a human being looks like. If an image doesn't exist showing exactly what the text to create it says, the generator will try to guess. It's while guessing that some horrendous mistakes take place. Let's just concentrate on the two examples shown here. In **Example A** the image seems photorealistic and perfectly rendered, until you notice the hands of the figure. They aren't right, looking wonky and missing fingers or having too many.

In **Example B** the amount of mistakes are even more appalling. Fist of all: what's supposed to be funny here? The text on the sign at the back is unreadable, the faces of the characters aren't even human, some have three eyes, and some don't even have a complete head, parts of limbs are missing, and we could go on and on. In other words, AI can't render flat line cartoons, unless it comes from CG-Animation or Anime. Oh, and doesn't understand humour.

Apparently mistakes can be fixed with the same AI generator used to create them. However, it will take many hours of trial and error to teach the generator what to do or not to do, hours better spent creating your own drawings with pen and pencil or a graphics tablet instead. ●

Example A

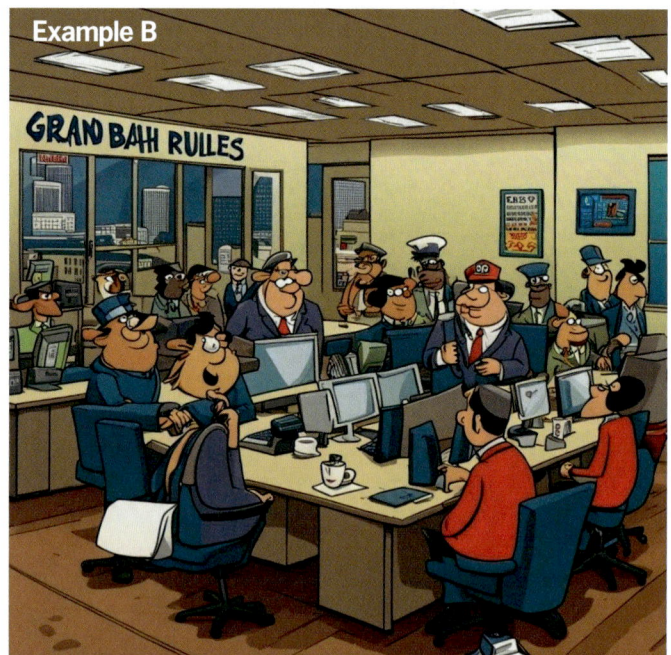

Example B

GRAND BAH RULLES

What AI can't do

Yin Xin He

Welcome to the dark and phantasmagorical dreamworld of this young Vietnamese illustrator.

FACING PAGE: *Un Chien Andalou*, acrylics on paper, 2023. Striking image from the Luis Buñuel and Salvador Dalí film of 1926.

BELOW: *The Age of Genius*, acrylics on paper, 2023. From the book 'Street of Crocodiles and other stories' by Bruno Schulz.

YIN XIN HE IS A YOUNG VIETNAMESE ARTIST and illustrator currently living in Germany. Her artwork is hard to categorise, being on the crossroads of conceptual surrealism with a certain fascination for the darker aspects of humanity.

"For me illustration isn't just visualising exactly what's shown in the texts but beyond that. My illustrations should reflect how I view the world, the knowledge I've absorbed in life. I like symbolism, metaphors and absurdity of the subconsciousness. With every artwork I take a step further into the unknown."

She hopes to illustrate many of the modern classic works of literature, including some of the more complex and darker ones.

We caught up with her recently for a short interview.

Did you always draw?

Yin Xin: I began to draw at a very early age, copying Donald Duck and Mickey from all the colouring books my mother bought me. I don't really draw every day, sometimes I spend days just to collect ideas and do more scribbles. It works better for me that way, to start an illustration with a statement first.

Were any other members of your family artistic?

Yin Xin: My father, he painted Chinese landscapes on bamboo blinds using watercolor/ink. But that was when I was a small child.

Where did you train?

Yin Xin: I first studied Product Design in my hometown in Vietnam, graduated but then began again in Germany in 2016. This time I studied design with my major in illustration.

89

What were your early influences?

Yin Xin: Probably Manga. When I was a teenager, I copied many manga characters. The internet wasn't popular back then in Vietnam so there wasn't much going on in my creative life, the reference I had in art was limited to fine art and manga only.

Did drawing come easily to you?

Yin Xin: I wasn't bad at learning to draw, I could pick it up faster than some people. But it didn't come easily, at the early learning stage I did everything less consciously, just copying what the mentors told me to do, without real understanding.

ABOVE: *Alex de Large*, acrylics on paper, 2023. Played by Malcolm McDowell in the 1976 movie 'A Clockwork Orange' by Stanley Kubrick.

FACING PAGE: *The Cabinet of Dr Caligari*, acrylics on paper, 2023. Inspired by the 1920 German silent horror movie.

Did you find it difficult to break into illustration?

Yin Xin: Concerning drawing, not too difficult, because I'd gathered some basic knowledge from the previous study. But to actually do something right, for example: anatomy... was more of a struggle. And after that I learn to convey messages through a more cinematographic aspect of illustration: composition, lighting, atmosphere... and above all finding my own style is the most difficult part, I think.

What sort of work did you do to begin with?

Yin Xin: My first job was between illustration and product design. I made drawings/watercolour illustrations to be printed on kitchenware: vases, plates, soup plates, cups... I've also illustrated a children's book but I haven't had an official commision in book illustration, not yet.

Did you always have a strong sense of the work you wanted to do?

Yin Xin: Since around 2019, I have found my path. Before that I was interested in many things, and college was very open for self-discovery. At the end of 2018 I tried my first book illustration project and that was the turning-point. I like projects that offer more room for interpretation.

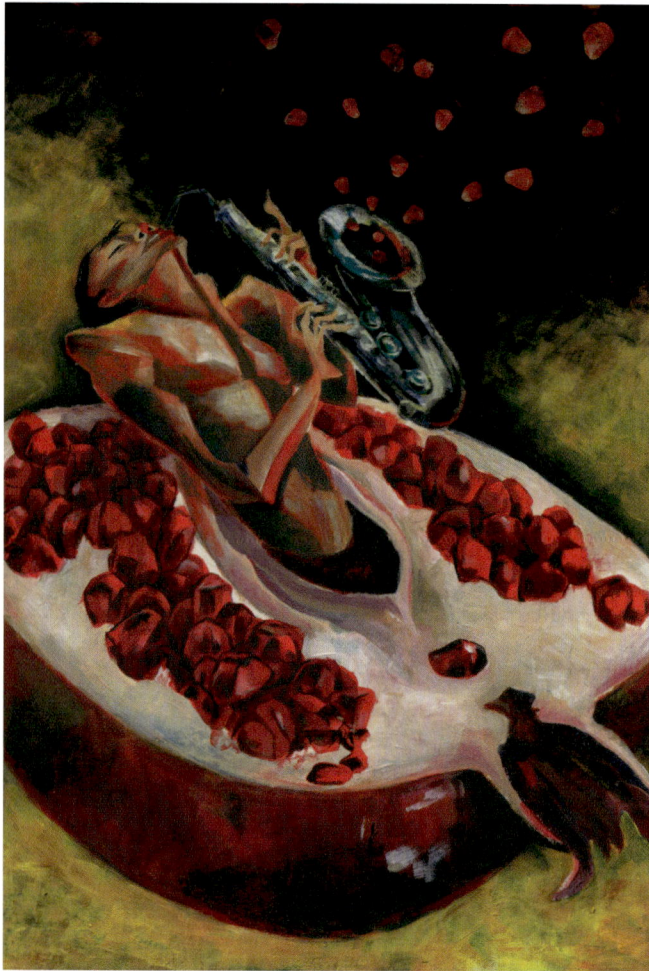

What medium (oils, acrylics, watercolour, etc.) do you use for your illustrations?

Yin Xin: I used to work with different materials, but for the last two years I've only focused on acrylics. The medium gives me the heaviness that I like to have for my work and also the textures that it's capable of creating. Then I would always add the last touches in Photoshop.

Do you prefer working in black and white or colour?

Yin Xin: For the moment I still enjoy working with colour. Each option gives out a different vibe. Black and white artworks offer a more detached feeling, more distant from the viewers. While colours have more power in manipulating our perception. Each colour correlates some certain meanings in our brain, red means danger or passion, green is freshness, youth... And if I want to say

certain things with an illustration, colour gives me more choices in expressing the idea.

Would you say it is easier to make illustration a career since you started?

Yin Xin: Not at all. There are not many publishing houses that invest in illustration for literature for adults. If I walk into a bookstore, most illustrated books are for children or young adults. There are comics or graphic novels for adults, but for the moment, I'm still trying to develop my potential for book illustration.

Do you think it is necessary for people wanting to work as professional illustrators to undertake a degree in illustration?

Yin Xin: I do. But for me it was less about the degree, but a place to meet people and exchange ideas. Art/Design schools are like a semi-trial before one gets to make it professionally. You have certain expectations, you have deadlines for each project, you get feedback... But if you mess up, it's not the end of the world. I believe college is a place where one's allowed the time to figure out what he/she really wants with less pressure. A degree is just to finalise your whole progress. I got to know my mentor from an 'artist talk' at my college, and that changed my whole path.

TOP LEFT: Illustration for the book *Steppenwolf*, acrylics on paper, 2020.

TOP RIGHT: *The Rise and Fall of an Heroic Era*, acrylics on paper, 2022.

FACING PAGE: *The Silent Hours of Motionless Madness*, acrylics on paper, 2023.

RIGHT: *The Hourglass Sanatorium*, acrylics on canvas, 2023. Inpsired by the movie directed by Wojciech Has (1973).

BELOW: Yin Xin, how can such a sweet person produce this disturbing artwork?

Have you any projects you are particularly pleased with?
Yin Xin: Not really, with each project I try and learn how to develop. If I choose not to go the safe way with a personal project, there would be more mistakes, but I also learn more when I risk more. And there are always illustrations that I love more than the others in the same project.

Have you any projects that turned into a nightmare?
Yin Xin: Yes, that was my first book illustration project, the short stories by Bruno Schulz. It was a complicated book for a first-timer like me.

What would you like to work on for the future?
Yin Xin: I would really like a chance to work on modern classic literature like 'Ulysses' and maybe 'Jabberwocky'

due to its absurdity. I really like psychology. If I were to receive a commision in that field, I would be pumped.

If you were starting out all over again—would you still make illustration your career?
Yin Xin: Yes, looking back on my whole journey to see all the highs and lows, I would still choose illustration as my career, anytime, any day. ●

———————————————————————

● *For more information on Yin Xin He you can visit her website: www.yinxinhe.de. She's also present on Instagram @yinxin-he*

Gallery: Tarzan and the Beastmaster by Russ Manning

THIS AND FOLLOWING PAGE: Already a popular artist on the *Tarzan* comic strip series, Russ Manning (1929-1981) was asked to create more Tarzan adventures for the European market in the 1970s. With asssistance from such artists as William Stout, Will Meugniot and Dave Stevens, among others, Manning brought forth 'Tarzan in the Land that Time Forgot', 'Tarzan and the Pool of Time', 'Tarzan in Savage Pellucidar' and 'Tarzan and the Beastmaster'. Of these, only the first two have been reprinted by Dark Horse (who represent ERB Inc. with the Tarzan comic book and strip series), but are now out of print. We leave you with some images from the last book of this European Tarzan series.

Images courtesy of Heritage Auctions - Tarzan © Edgar Rice Burroughs Inc.

Tarzan © Edgar Rice Burroughs Inc.